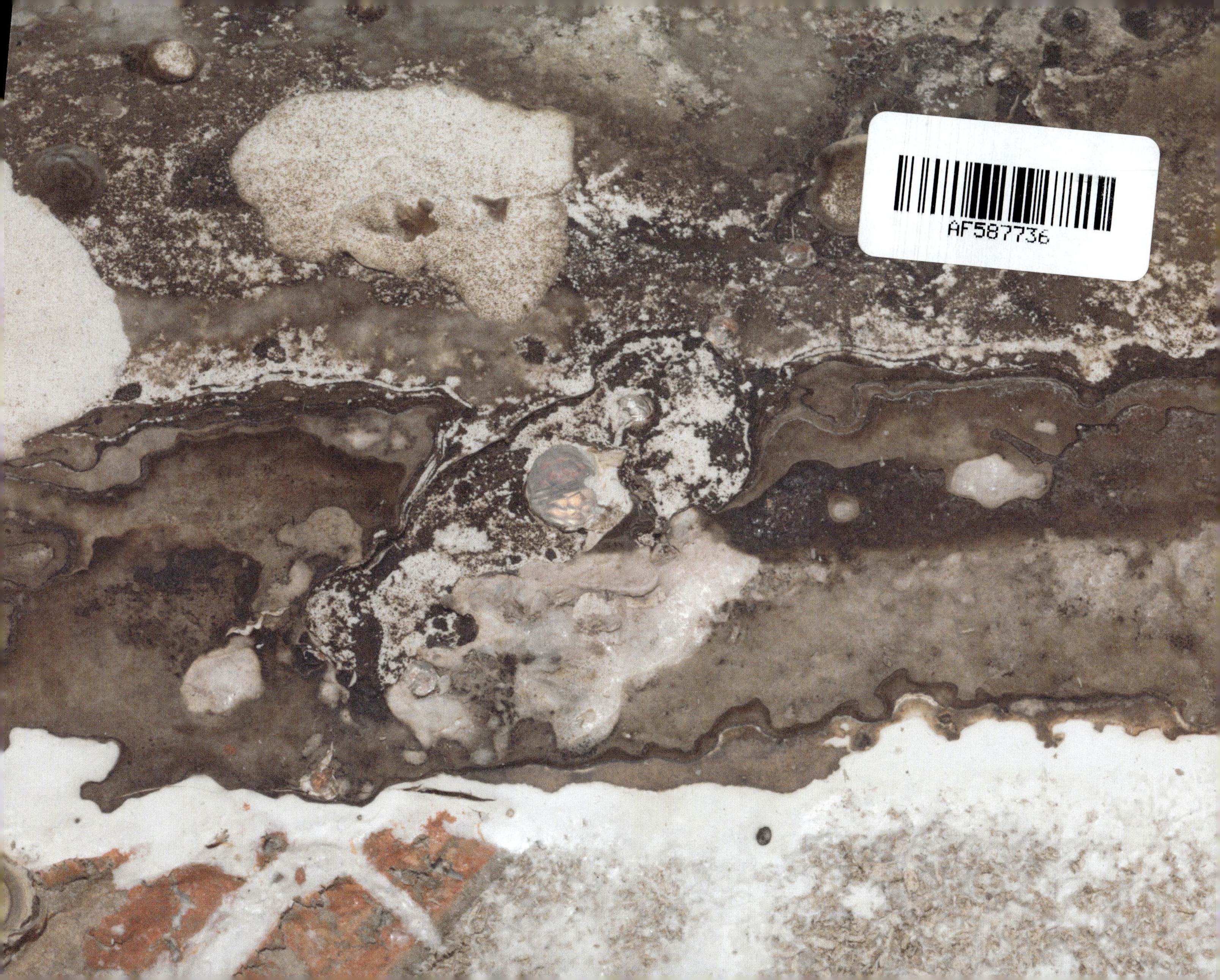

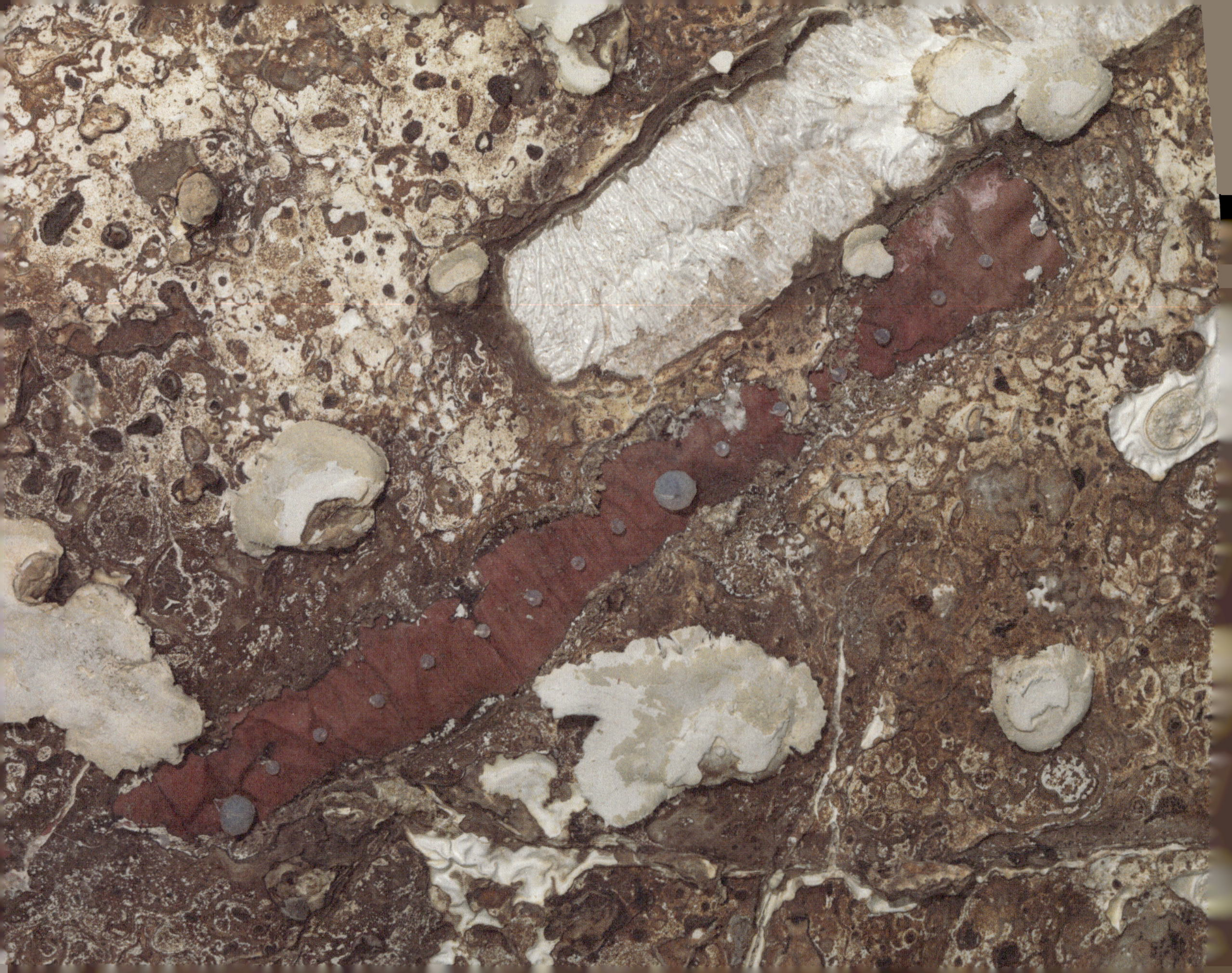

DAFNE PHONO

NOUR MOBARAK'S

dafne phono

Wendy's Subway

CONTENTS

PREFACE

Nour Mobarak

Dafne Phono is a multimedia adaptation of the first opera, *Dafne*, written and composed in 1598 by Ottavio Rinuccini and Jacopo Peri. Adapted from the poet Ovid's fable, the plot revolves around the hubris of the god Apollo, and the entrapment of his beloved, Dafne. As punishment for boasting of his conquests, Cupid and Venus seek revenge on Apollo by shooting two arrows. The first makes Apollo fall in love with Dafne, the daughter of the river god. The second makes Dafne revile him; she escapes his grip by transmogrifying into a laurel tree. Apollo, spurned, turns the laurel tree into the emblem of his eternal love for Dafne, who remains forever trapped—the sign of his victory. In *Dafne Phono*, this myth becomes something of a parable for a modern history of language and hegemony.

In *Dafne Phono*, I reflect on the relationship between power dynamics and physical matter as they are differentially experienced—as nested, fractal, inter-causal, invisible and visible, felt and empirical, metamorphic. The history of opera, with its own hyper-sensorial ambitions, lent itself nicely to this project, which attempts to trace various bodies and their operations within nature, myth, empire, and language, and how those structures in turn affect the bodies that constitute them. In its early years, opera was a thought experiment to explore what it would mean for music to be composed from one voice. As opera historian Nicolas Slonimsky explains, the innovation of opera "consisted in reducing music to a clearly outlined single voice…It was a state of musical entropy, in which the underlying matter remains stable in its solidity."[1] *Dafne Phono* became a self-generating project, offering manifold material with which to form the web of my own interior logic, but it originates in my curiosity around the

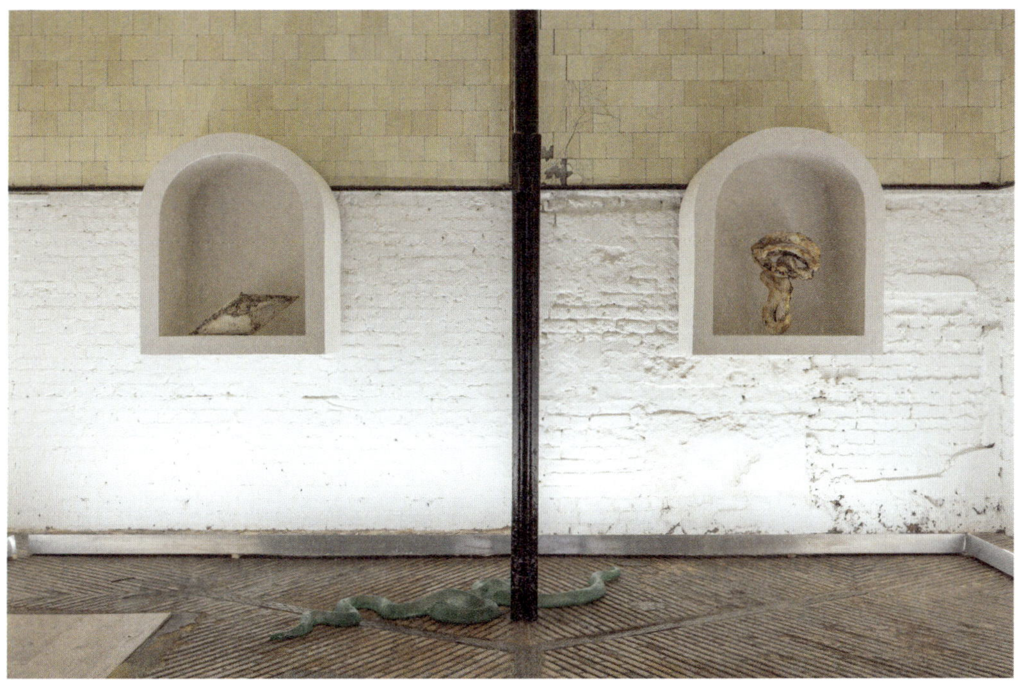

affective and effective human voice, and how our bodies are molded into material instruments. I wanted to explore how communication and sense-perception shift as our spoken phonetic palette narrows through the homogenizing, hegemonic forces of monolingualism, assimilation, and globalization. In *Dafne Phono* I adapted the sixteenth-century libretto into six languages, chosen for their morphonological complexity, with the aim of creating an opera with the widest palette of vocal sounds.

Dafne Phono considers how human languages define systems of knowledge and cognition, as well as the affective quality of the human voice as it speaks these languages and otherwise "voices." As languages develop, sounds are assigned meaning to form words within language systems that determine our realities. As one civilization and economy colonizes another, the colonized language and its morphonology are altered—sometimes altogether lost—while the colonizing language absorbs it into digestible fragments. In *Dafne Phono*, the music is mostly composed by making micro-samples of the language recordings I made not only for their narrative content, but also for their sounds, and arranging them musically (or, at least, with primary attention to sound). I listened for moments of breakdown and groove. Divorcing speech sounds from meaning—a strategy used before me by many sound artists and poets, from John Cage to Kurt Schwitters—allows the listener to "decreate" language, and to consider the other, alternate worldviews that can be built from reassembling speech sounds, or phonemes. The term "decreation" is also fitting in a discussion of the material properties of saprophytic fungi, a species of fungi that live by decomposing dead organic matter. These are the kinds of fungi I mostly use to sculpt with. Questions of language, repetition, decay, civilization, power, and metamorphosis emerge in this work, which interweaves biological processes with the transformation of speech.

The work explores the voice as material, creating spatialized sound and language objects out of the organic substance of mycelium. In its sculptural form, *Dafne Phono* is installed as a staged tableau comprising fifteen mycelium sound sculptures. Mycelium is fungi, and it is the root form of the mushroom. Its biological composition is rhizomatic, repeating, expanding and proliferating through a cycle of decomposition and recomposition—much like human language. Its

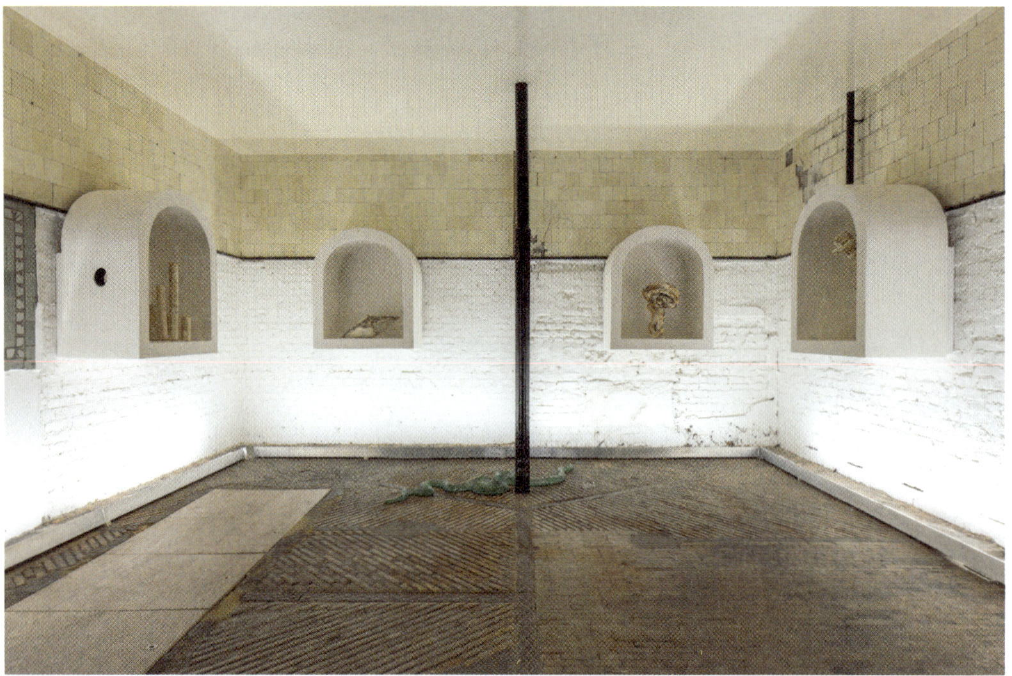

branching network of filamentous cells called hyphae create a dense web that can take over its substrate, be dried out, petrified, and last for quite some time, much like wood. In the installation, the large-scale mycelium forms embody each of the opera's characters (inlaid with glass beads, as early operatic convention required), save for the slain Python, which is made of plastic and plaster, and Ovid, who appears as a vacuum-suctioned oval void in the wall.

The music from *Dafne* has been lost, but the libretto remains. In *Dafne Phono*, the original opera's libretto formed the basis for a series of operations of translation that divert the arguably Apollonian romance language of opera—Apollonian insofar as it adopts the language of the oppressive force—to give voice to a polyphony of phonetically complex languages selected on the basis of the richness of their morphophonology, that is, together these languages present the widest palette of vocal sounds. They include: Abkhaz from Abkhazia, San Juan Quiahije Eastern Chatino from modern-day Oaxaca, Silbo Gomero from the Canary Islands, and Taa (West !Xoon dialect), which is spoken by the San People of modern-day Namibia and Botswana. Ovid's native Latin and Rinuccini and Peri's original Italian are also used. Each of the opera's six characters—Dafne, Apollo, Venus, Eros, Ovid, and the Chorus—speaks their lines in a different language. Only Apollo's speech remains in the original Italian.

When researching and selecting these languages, my interest was primarily formal—I sought sounds, but did not intend on choosing any language for its rarity or indigeneity. The prompt, however, led me to recording some of the oldest and most rapidly disappearing languages on Earth. While I am not a linguist, I could not help but observe that the trend this points to is toward a narrowing functionality of the sensorial, organic human body. Reports that we are also losing manual dexterity due to pervasive use of screen technology seems to correlate.

The translation process took some time. Finding native speakers of the languages I wanted to record meant cold-emailing academics or writing to users on YouTube who had worked with speakers of these languages before me. After many non-replies and dead-ends, I was eventually able to find the right voices. Recording people often meant having to travel to them myself, and so I did. I myself am a vocalist, and have been

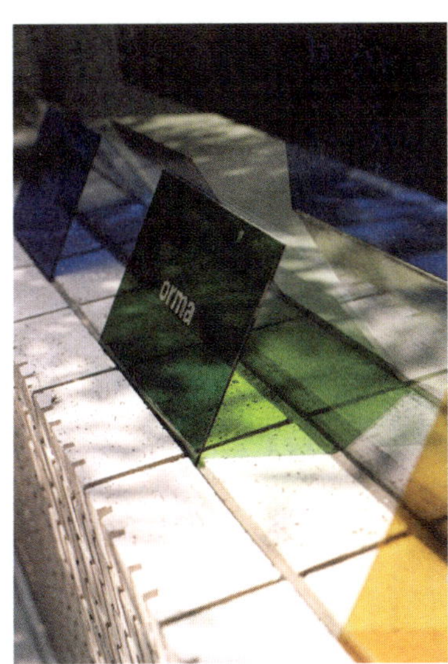

interested in vocal extension and the potential of the voice since my teenage years. The vocal palette of romance languages, I noticed, was very limited. English, while having a wide variety of pronunciations, generally shares similar phonological palettes between dialects. It uses roughly forty-five phonemes, or language sounds. The Taa language has roughly 107 phonemes, with the addition of two phonemic tones, or pitch levels. As of 2011, there were only 2,500 native speakers of Taa remaining. In order to create this work, then, I spent several months finding speakers of the Taa language, specifically the !Xoon dialect, by calling and texting the few phone numbers a linguist had passed on to me until someone replied. After a few weeks someone finally did, and they shared their geolocation coordinates. I traveled to Eastern Namibia, in the Kalahari Desert, to camp with the San people and translate and record their parts on site. I traveled, too, to record Chatino, a language spoken by the Zacatepec Chatino people in the mountains of inland Oaxaca. The Abkhaz, Silbo Gomero, Italian, and Latin were spoken in less remote regions, so I worked at a distance with local collaborators to translate and record.

The three *Dafne Phono* libretti in this book present each stage of the translation process. In the first libretto, Rinuccini's original Renaissance Italian is printed in the left-most column, and translations into each of the other languages are laid out alongside. The second libretto takes all of these translations from Italian and translates them into English, but this time, literally, word for word, to present each language's syntax and precise word choice, rather than privileging overarching meaning. Through this literal procedure, unitary words are emphasized over comprehensive phrasal meaning, in the hopes of evincing some of the cognitive, linguistic realities created by each language. These translations are abundant and imperfect, revealing the inevitable slippages, mistranslations, discrepancies that emerged through process; they give rise to a kind of tone poetics. In the final phase, represented in the third libretto, the process-generated abstractions of the word-for-word translation of the previous stage are translated into Greek, as the full installation of *Dafne Phono* was first presented in Piraeus.

When it has been installed, performed segments of the second libretto are projected as subtitles—in English in exhibitions in Los Angeles and New York—while the English and Greek of the second and third libretto served as subtitles in Piraeus. As a sculptural installation, each of the fifteen characters broadcast their lines from their own sound monitor, implanted within the hollowed sculptures-cum-speakers. Mycelium's material density allows the voice to bleed through, creating a filtered, embodied effect. This speaks back to the original conditions of presentation of the 1598 opera: The theatrical stage designer, architect, artist, military designer, and Italian ice cream inventor Bernardo Buontalenti conceived not only the costumes for the opera's production, which was commissioned by the extravagant Medici family, but also the titular Buontalenti Grotto (the "Grotta di Buontalenti"), accessed from the gardens of Florence's Uffizi. The grotto housed statues of Greek mythical gods and goddesses like Apollo and Ceres, sculptures nestled in the uneven and organic walls of the cave where stalagmites and concretions formed. In *Dafne Phono*, the mycelium as substrate creates a visual echo of Buontalenti's eccentric and visionary work with natural geological formations, which was undertaken over the course of thirty years, from 1557 to 1587. *Dafne* would be performed at the nearby Palazzo Pitti a decade later.

The 1598 production was staged in the Sala dei Nicchie, or, Room of the Niches, and is part of the oldest structure of the fifteenth-century building, located above the main entrance to the Palazzo. It is so named after the niches that contain classical statues of many of the Gods who make up the cast of characters in the first opera. A doubling was present at the moment of *Dafne's* first performance that I wanted to attend to when making this work, to reflect on what seemed to me to be a sort of proto-postmodern gesture. When I presented *Dafne Phono* in Piraeus, Greece, I simultaneously showed miniatures of each of the works, set into niches, at Rodeo's gallery space in London. This show, titled *Gods' Facsimiles*, set the stage for *Dafne Phono*. Another extension of this work was the piece *Dafne Phos*, presented at Amant in New York in the 2023 group show *Siren (some poetics)*. For this I took all the words for "footprint" present in the new libretto and had them etched into differently colored glass. As the sun passed through the glass panels, the shadow of the word would project onto the surface behind it.

I am a performer, and I see *Dafne Phono*—the libretti, the installation, the video—as an extension of my performance practice. I am concerned that our species is slowly narrowing the spectrum of variation of human voice's sonic expression and how we listen. I play with these ideas when I use my own body to make work. This narrowing is a result of many intersecting forces, such as the suppression and endangerment of cultures and languages through imperial and colonial expansion, which resembles the narrowing of Earth's species due to capitalist and colonial resource extraction. At the human and planetary scales, the operations of the sensual, organic body are fractally shrinking. Yet sounds and sensations can sometimes communicate in ways semantics cannot. With *Dafne Phono*, I wanted to outsource my voice to the voices of many, and to the bodies of other species. Because, as the Chorus sings: "Tyu^{H} u^{J} ntyqya^{J} qa^{E} niya^{J} re^{c} / ntqan^{G} sqyu^{c} ke^{A} lon^{H} re^{c}, neq^{c} nkaq^{E} yka^{J} nkqa^{G}."[2]

NOTES

1 Nicolas Slonimsky, foreword to Laura Diane Kuhn, *Baker's Dictionary of Opera* (New York: Schirmer Books, 2000).

2 *Dear beautiful more looks this, saw seed rock face this, into leaves tree green*

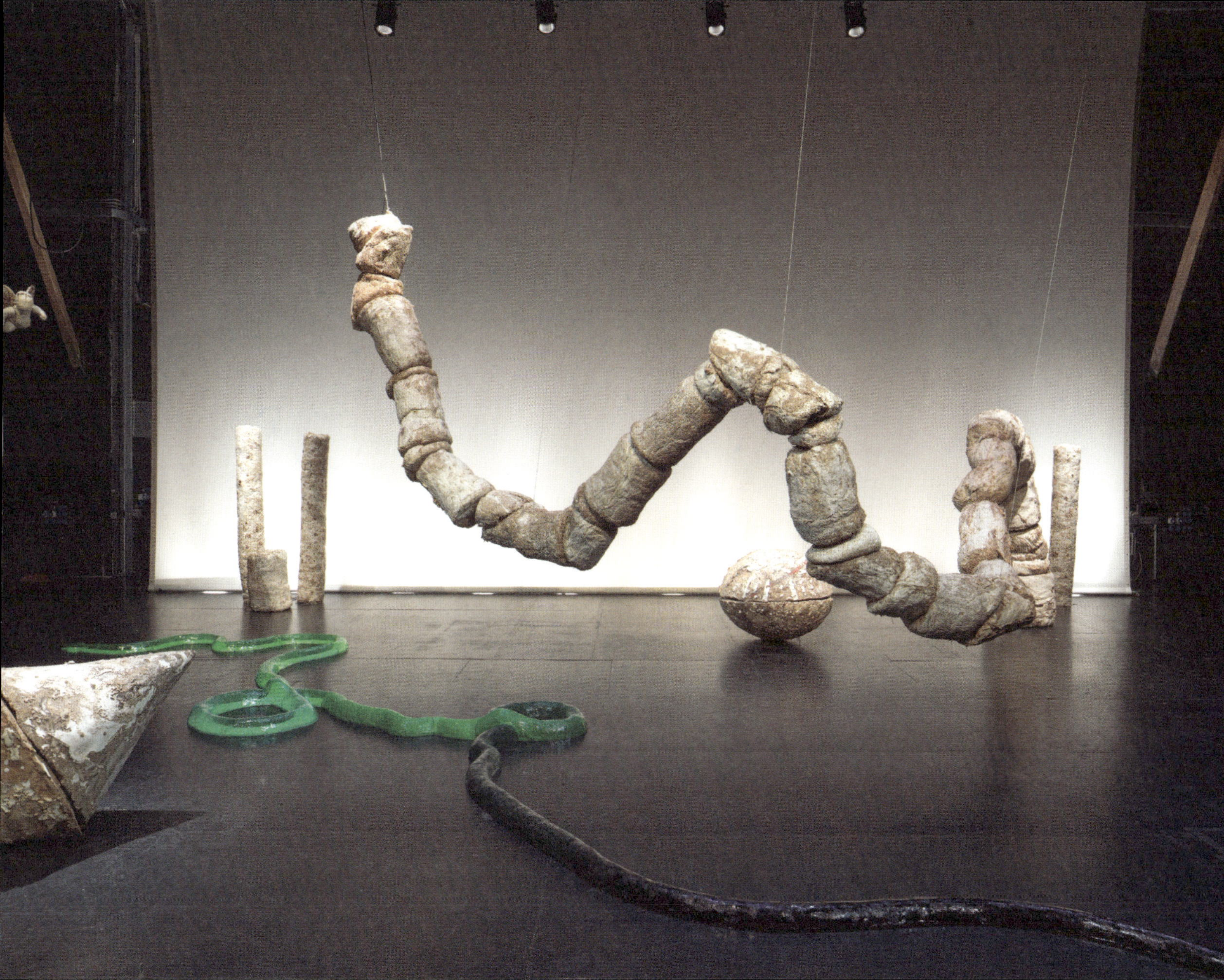

TRANSLATION AND METAMORPHOSIS

Anahid Nersessian

There is a belief among psychoanalysts that the very first object we encounter is our mother's voice. It comes to us from outside the womb, a percussive force vibrating through the amniotic ocean. Unlike the mother's blood, oxygen, and food, it is not something we can share in effortlessly. It is beyond us, and we want it. Desire is born before we are.

Dafne Phono is an opera, an elegy, an experiment, and a ceremonial recovery of the voice (or *phono*) as a material object. It writes over, against, and through the primary texts of Western civilization, as Nour Mobarak's sculptures quite literally metabolize these texts, devouring without destroying them. These elemental forms are hollow within. They conceal the speakers from which the *dramatis personae* speak, and they are made of mycelium, creating a fungal tissue those voices must pass through, their density, pitch, and tenor molded and changed. The result is a multimedia, multispecies work of art that undoes fixed categories of the artificial and the organic—as well as gender, race, power, music, poetry, and the visual arts—dissolving their limits in a teeming, sensuous profusion of sound and image.

In 1598 the world's first opera, *Dafne*, was composed by Jacopo Peri and Ottavio Rinuccini, who based his libretto on an earlier one: "Combattimento di Apollo col serpente Pitone." The "Combattimento" had been performed nine years earlier as an *intermezzo* during the marriage celebration of Ferdinando I de' Medici and Cristina di Lorena. *Intermezzi*—lavish theatrical performances staged on extravagant sets—were a favorite entertainment of the aristocracy, particularly on special occasions. They involved song, speech, and music but not all at the same time.

With *Dafne*, Peri found a way to keep his performers singing throughout the performance using a new style called *stile recitativo*, or recitative.

Peri's goal, in his words, was "to make a simple test of what the song of our time was capable of."[1] The dynamics of recitative, however, are far from simple. They involve the production of a calculated dissonance between the vocal melody and the harmonic substructure of its musical accompaniment. Instead of following the composition's melody, the singer recites the libretto according to the rhythms and accents of spoken language. By playing with the conflict and consonance between the libretto and the score, Peri found, he said, "a new harmony" that might capture the full range of human emotion.

Dafne is both a novelty and a mimicry. It is based on a story from Ovid's *Metamorphoses*, about the sun deity Apollo and the nymph Daphne. After defeating the dragon-snake Python, Apollo insults Cupid, the "little, naked, and blind" god of love, by telling him to leave bows and arrows to big gods like him. To prove his own superior strength, Cupid shoots Apollo with an arrow that causes him to love Daphne, and Daphne with an arrow that causes her to hate Apollo. Apollo chases Daphne; Daphne runs away. In Ovid's telling, she begs her father, a river god, for help. He turns her into a laurel tree, which Apollo then claims as his own. "Always on my golden brow," Rinuccini's Apollo says, "will your leaves and branches make a garland"—a reference to the Greco-Roman custom of using laurel wreaths as a symbol of triumph.

Ovid's *Metamorphoses* includes over two-hundred and fifty myths of transformation. An outstanding number of them are stories about sexual violence. Daphne becomes a tree and the nymph Syrinx, fleeing from the satyr Pan, is changed into a cluster of reeds, which Pan then uses to make his pipes. Another nymph, Arethusa, turns into a stream to escape the river god Alpheus, who, undeterred, forcibly joins his waters to hers. "The underside of culture," as the literary critic Fredric Jameson once put it, "is blood, torture, death, and terror."[2] Ovid's poem is an example of this tragic interdependence and a requiem for its victims.

Dafne Phono, then, is in the Ovidian tradition. By translating Rinuccini's Italian libretto into Latin, Abkhaz, Chatino, Silbo Gomero, and !Xoon (Taa dialect), Mobarak emphasizes the link between culture and colonization, and how one language can act as an invasive species, making it impossible for others to exist. When these languages sound together during performance, they exponentiate the power Peri attributed to his recitative: that of using dissonance, or musical disharmony, to capture an otherwise inaudible emotional timbre or tone.

What linguists call the Sapir-Whorf hypothesis holds that the structure of a language determines its speakers' perceptions. If Mobarak's translation process has created an opera with the widest palette of human vocal sounds, it has also created not just a clash of aural frequencies but—with its riot of whistles, clicks, consonants, and diphthongs—a collision of worlds. Each note acts as an acoustic cue, activating distinct emotional and cognitive responses in the listener with the same immediacy and intensity as a visual image.

Dafne Phono begins with the lone voice of Ovid, intoning the opera's prologue in his native Latin. He speaks from a hole in the wall, with a vacuum suctioning air positioned behind it. This Ovid-void, which really does suck the air out of the room, is the voice of literary authority and of the Roman imperium. It is swiftly overtaken by Italian and Silbo Gomero, a whistling language used by inhabitants of La Gomera in the Canary Islands. Because Silbo Gomero emulates Spanish phonology, it represents both a history of colonial aggression (Spain settled the Canary Islands between 1402 and 1496) and a creative response to its strictures—the construction of an alternative reality alongside an unlivable one.

The first part of Mobarak's libretto makes, to use Peri's phrase, a new harmony out of disparate sonic and syntactical elements; the second part dismantles that harmony. Here, Mobarak has translated her Latin, Abkhaz, Chatino, Silbo Gomero, and Taa texts into modern English, meaning that the resulting script has now been translated twice, first from the Italian of 1598 and then once again. The result is a suite of haunting motifs that expose the incommensurabilities between one language and the next as well as the expressive limits of language per se.

"Per te," Rinuccini's Chorus tells Apollo, "vive e per te gode quanto scerne occhio mortale, o rettor del carro eterno"—*Through you the mortal eye enlivens and enjoys all that it sees, o ruler of the eternal chariot*. Apollo is not only the god of the sun but also of poetry and art, a civilizing force that supercharges everything with a new liveliness and beauty. But already, once these lines are translated, their original meaning begins to disintegrate and a more ominous tonality to surface. "Through you lives and enjoys the mortal eye all that it discerns," goes the English, a syntactically perplexed statement whose lack of clarity casts a shadow on the sun god's might. In Abkhaz, the phrase "the mortal eye" becomes "the death's eye," while the translation from Chatino gives us "Through happy you came light earth everything discerns to seed rock face mortal."

The coolly subversive power of translation is especially evident in the Chorus's account of Daphne becoming a tree. The Italian text, rendered into English, praises the "new marvels" of Daphne's transformation, admiring how her blonde hair turns "into tree-like fronds," and how "the foot that just now ran fast and loose" is suddenly "buried in the ground, sprouting branches and leaves." But in English the Chatino lines become almost nonsensical, as if to dramatize Daphne's loss of the ability to speak for herself. With her "hanging hair blonde hair" changed "into leaves tree green," and her "loose fast foot…buried inside soil sprouting thing branches and leaves," Daphne is less a tree than a compound of nouns and adjectives. The !Xoon text, put (again) into English, finds her footprints "disappeared."

On the page at least, the Western idiom is losing its grip over sense, while a new collective language—elliptical, skeptical, strange—takes its place. You could call that language "poetry," but it is not Apollo's kind. The *décalage*, or misfit, between each of Mobarak's languages, and between the original text of *Dafne* and its various translations, leaves open a space where unexpected images, thoughts, ideas, and intuitions can emerge. Translation, of course, is also a metamorphosis, a change from one form into another. In *Dafne Phono*, it becomes a material operation on the substance of reality itself, a sacred procedure that, like the magic that saturates Ovid's world, can shift life into death, love into cruelty, hymns of the powerful into the complaint of the weak.

In ancient Greece, theater actors wore masks called *prosopon*, which, in the most basic sense, means "face." But the true reach of the word is much broader, for a *prosopon* is not merely a face but an extension and expression of the essence of a person. Etymologically, it seems to derive from the Greek *pros*, "to," "toward," or "at," and *ōpa*, "face" or "eye." A *prosopon*, then, is the means by which something is presented outward, to someone else. For the Greeks, a painter's brush was a *prosopon*, for with it she makes concrete and visible to others what is interior to herself; a sculptor's clay, or her mycelium, is a *prosopon* too.

What Mobarak has done with *Dafne Phono* is restore Daphne's voice to her through the *prosopon* of multiple voices, each speaking its own language. The restoration is at once partial and superabundant. Daphne's metamorphosis cannot be undone or her nymph's body resurrected, just as the histories of violence of which it is both allegory and instance cannot be run backwards. But the silence that accompanies her transformation can be exploded, upset, made full by the beautiful noise of human plurality. It is this song we are invited to hear.

NOTES

1 Quoted in Anthony M. Cummings, *Music in Golden-Age Florence, 1250–1750* (Chicago: University of Chicago Press, 2023), 246.

2 Fredric Jameson, *Postmodernism, or, The Cultural Logic of Late Capitalism* (Durham, NC: Duke University Press, 1992), 5.

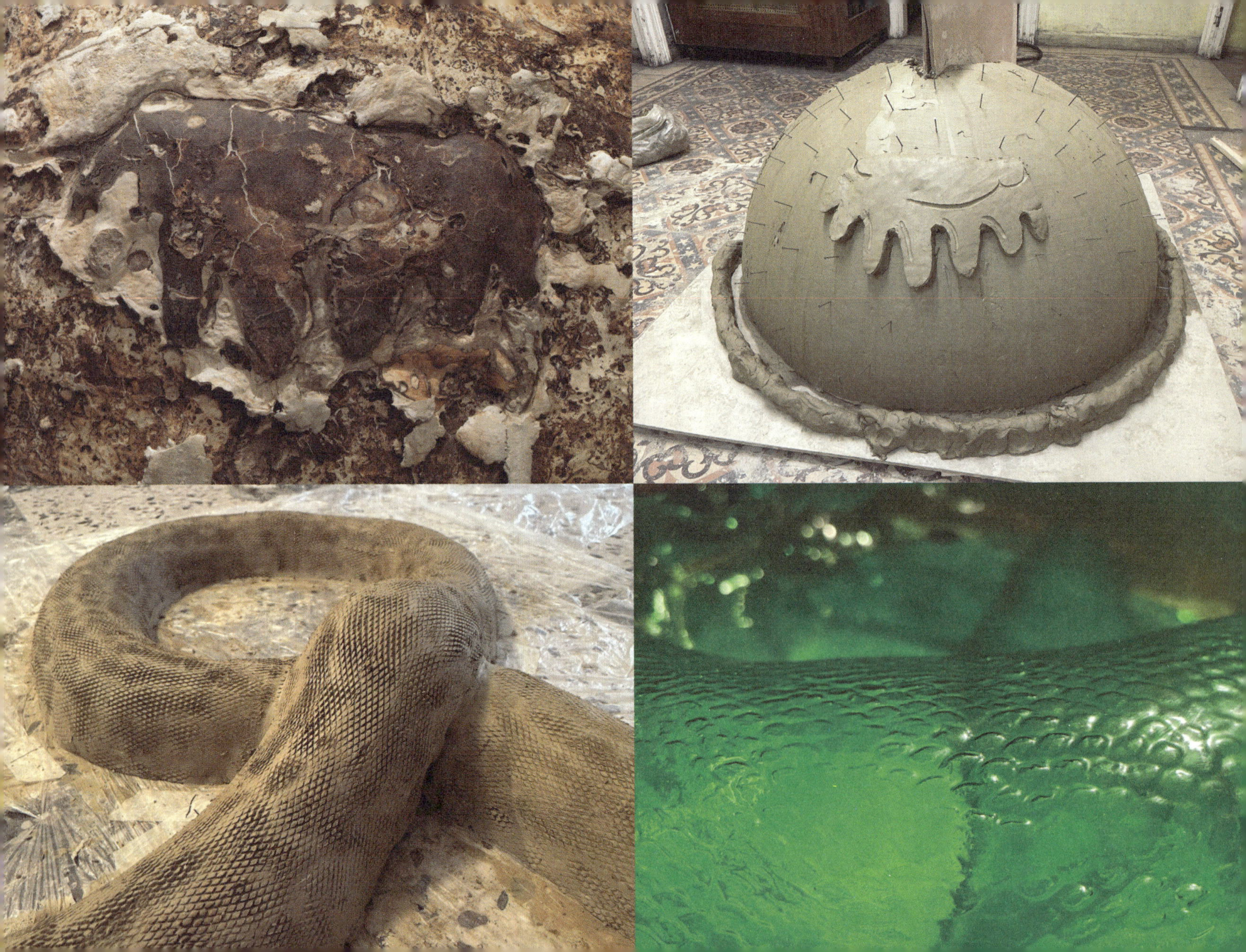

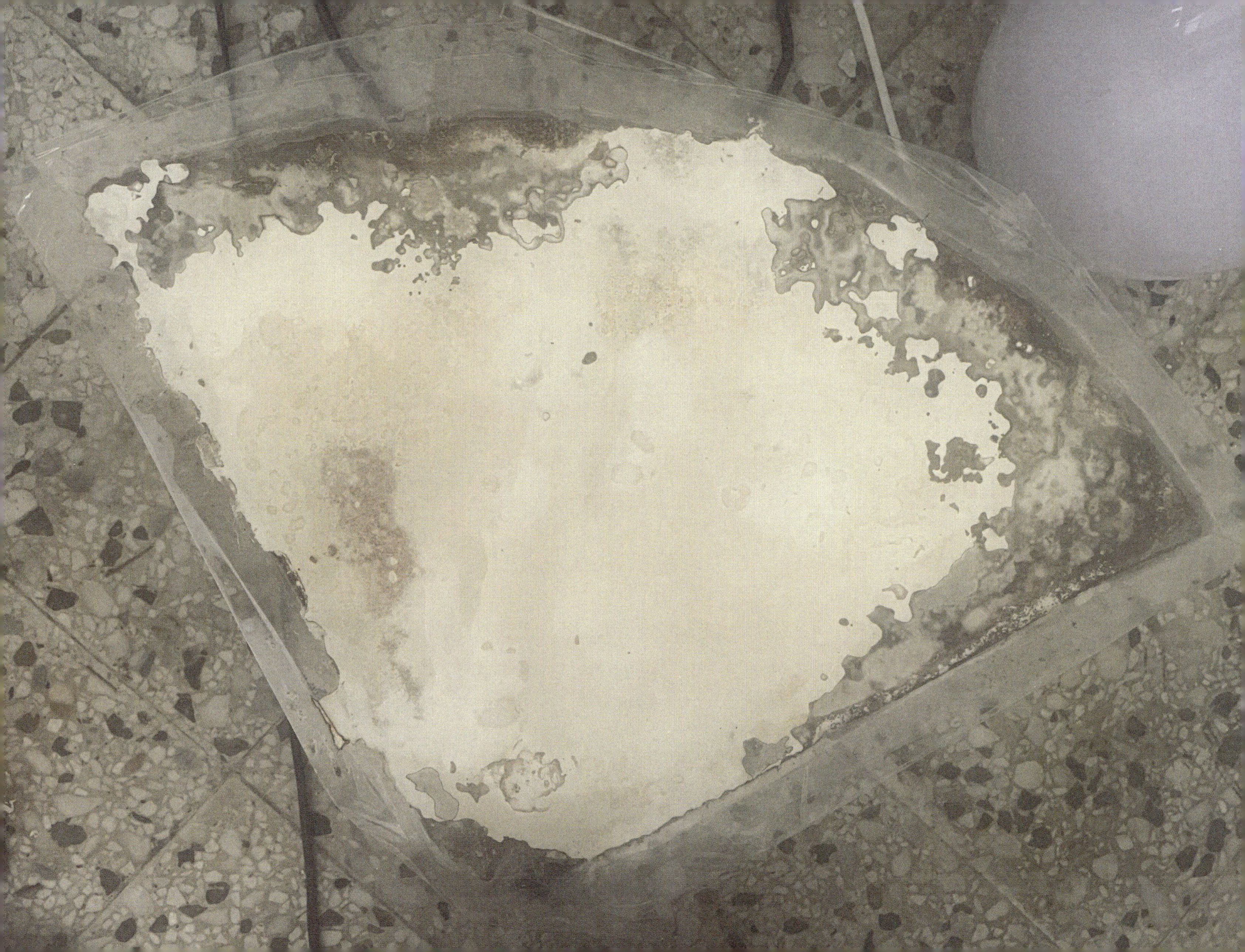

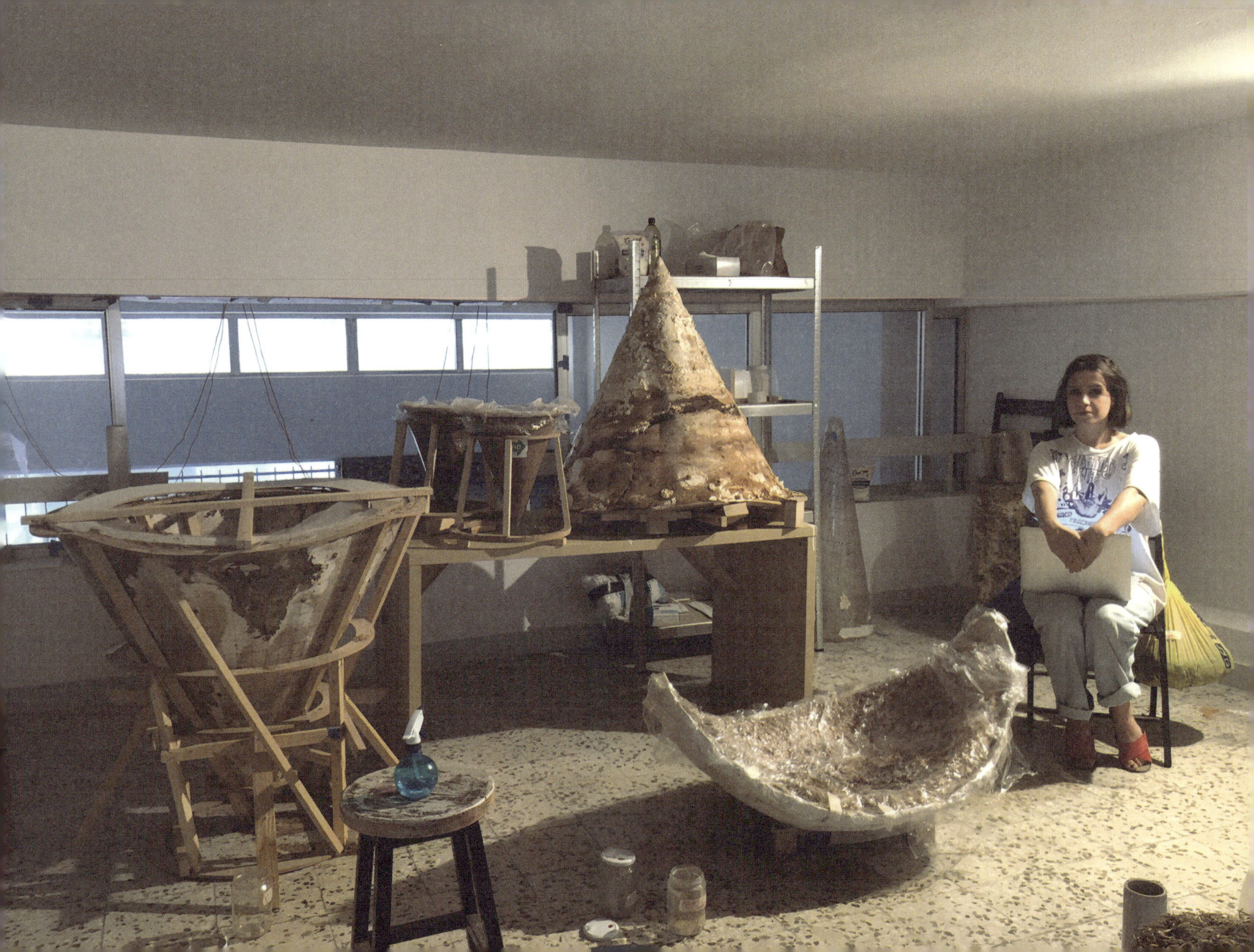

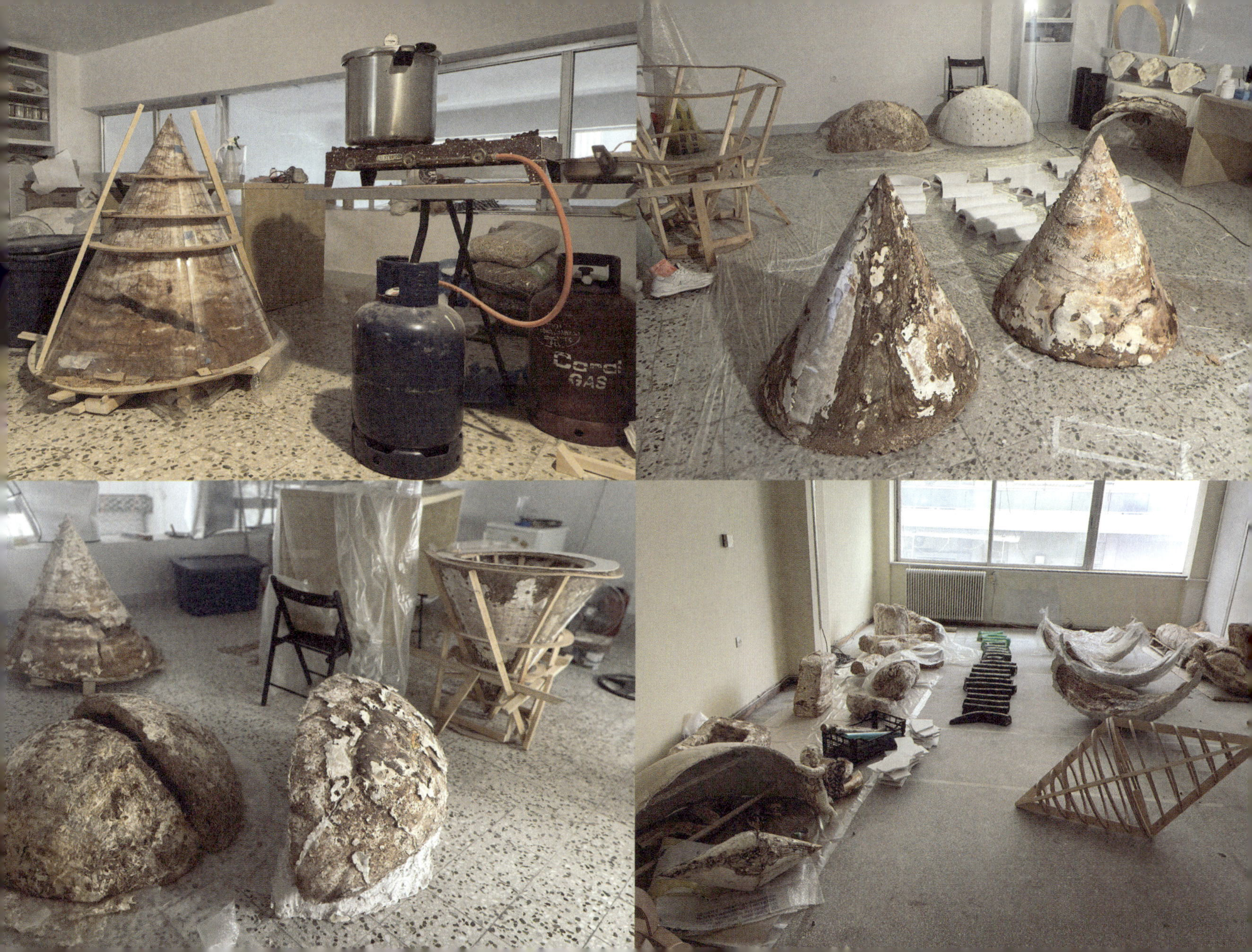
GAS

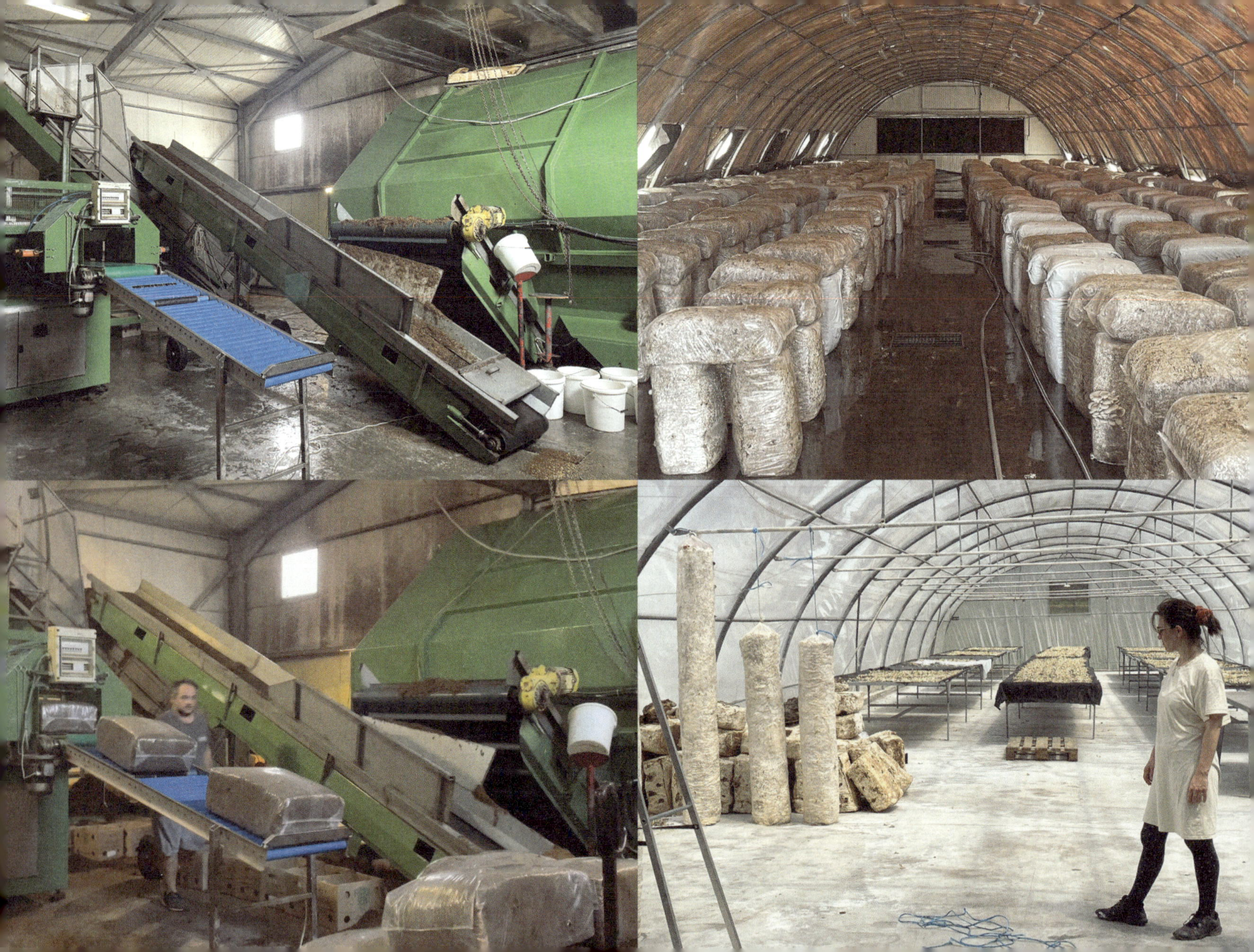

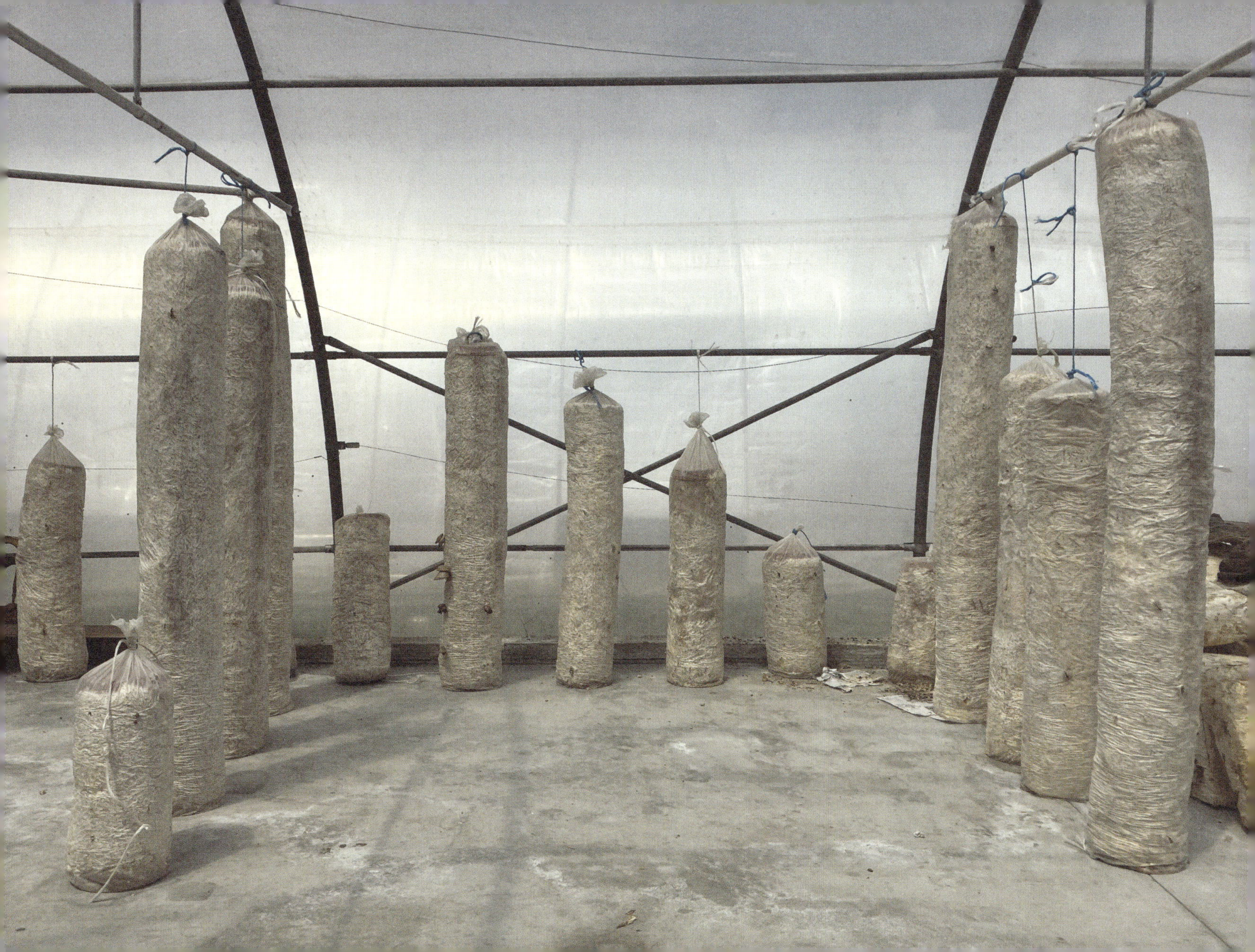

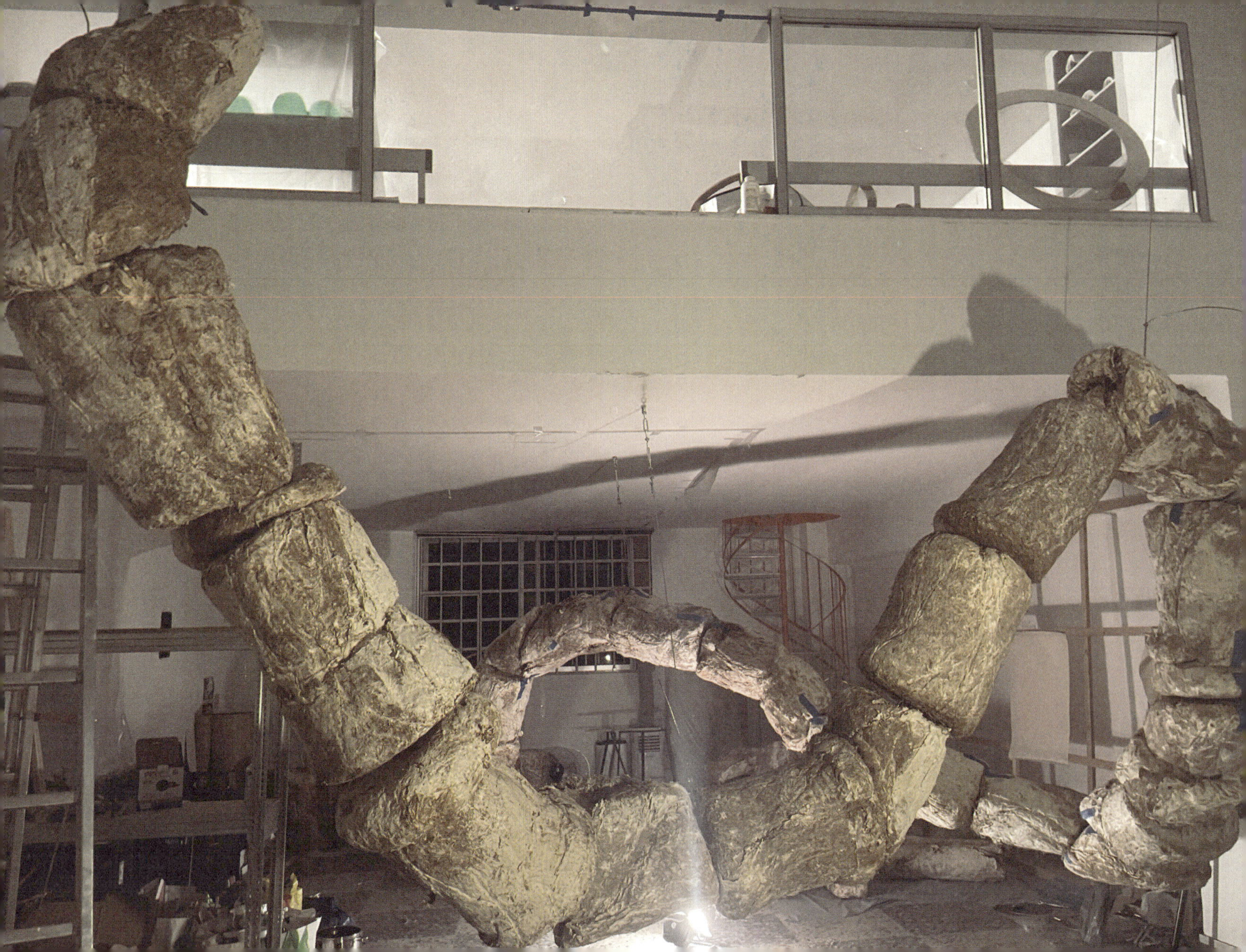

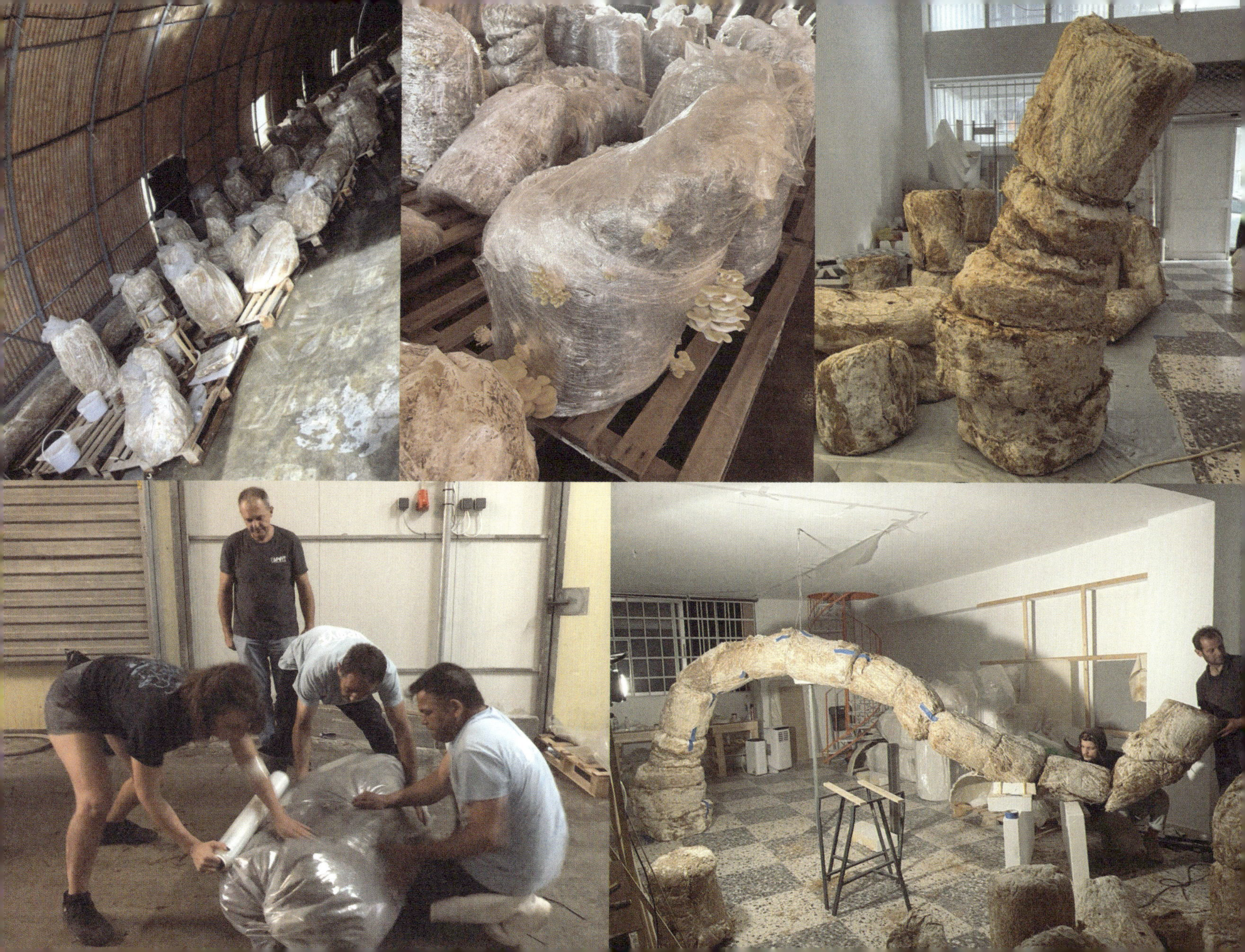

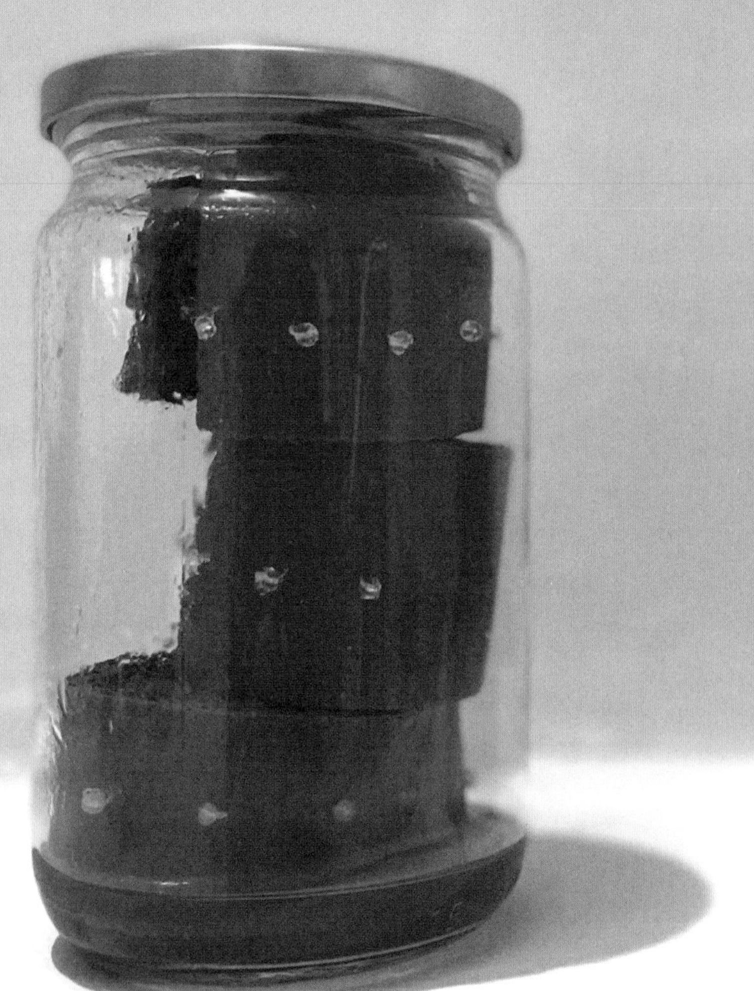
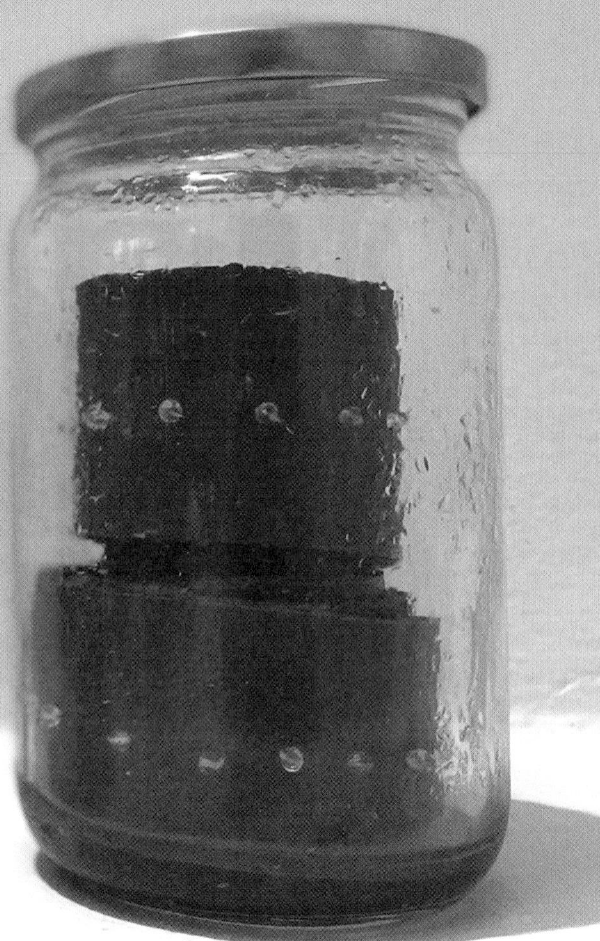

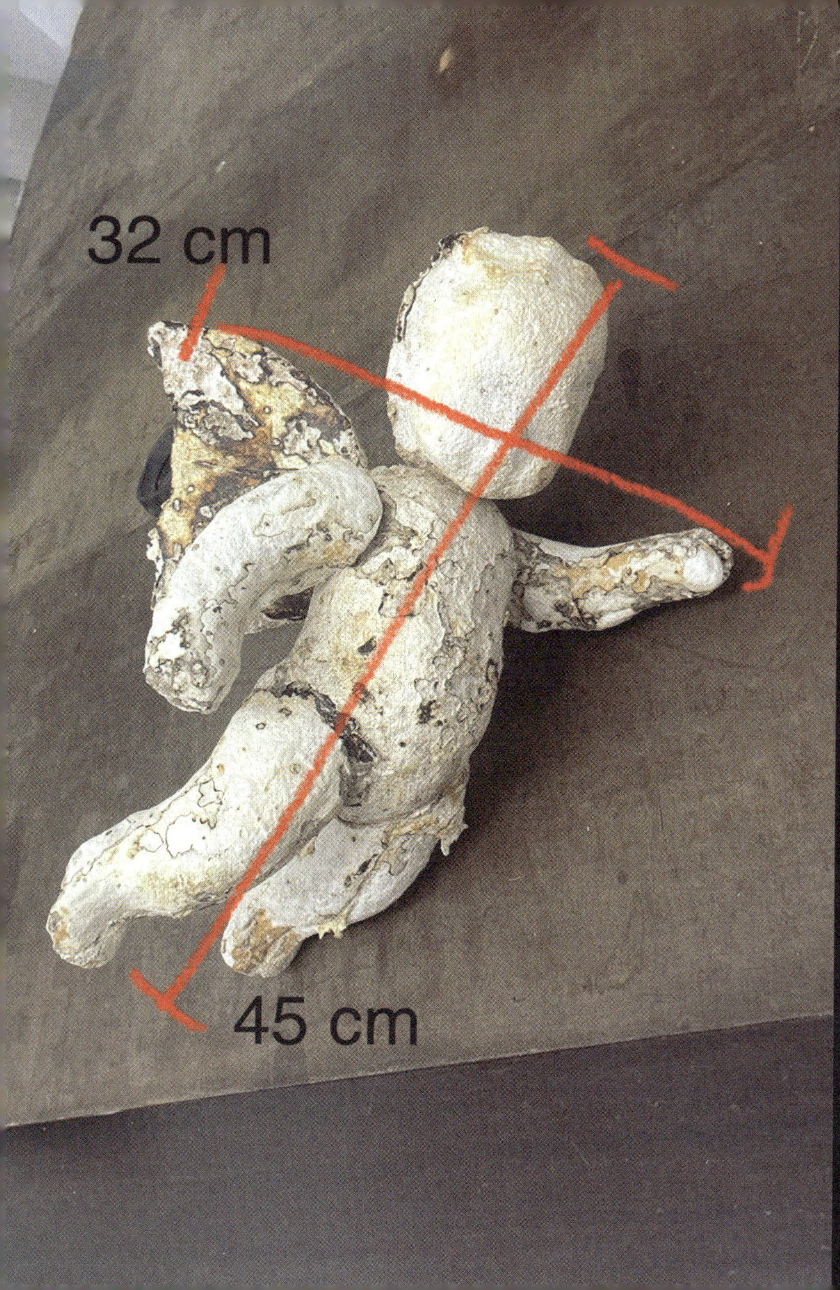

32 cm

45 cm

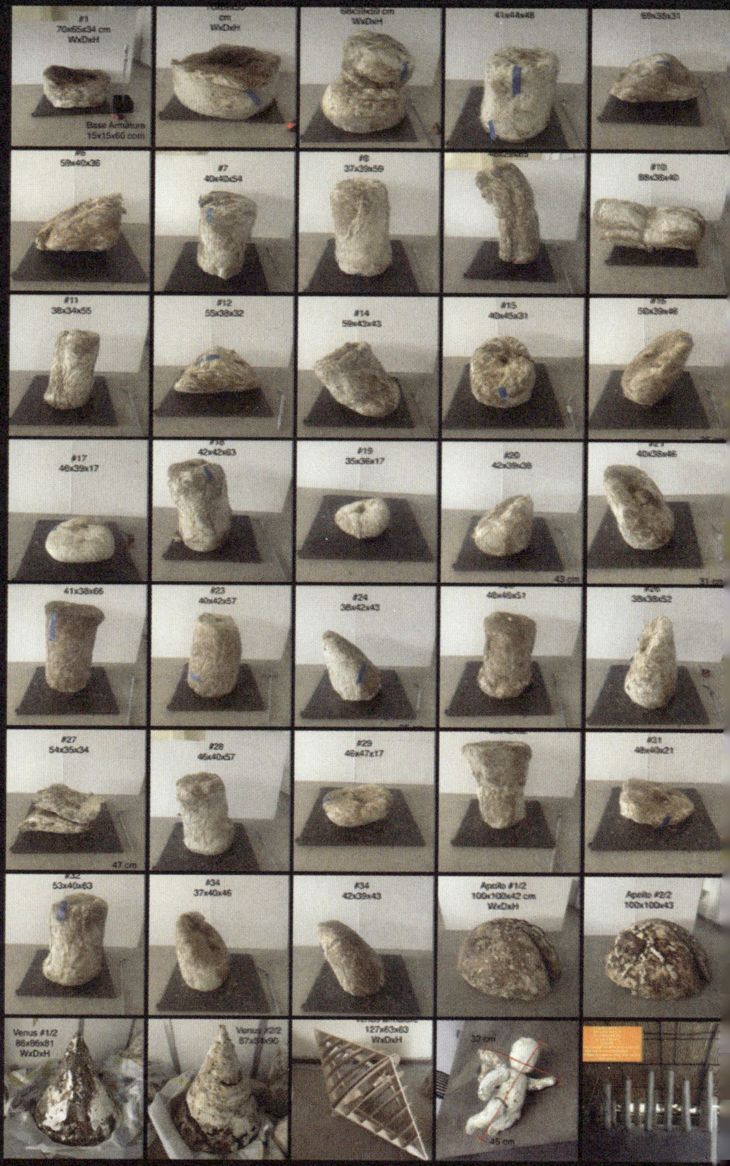

#1
70x65x34 cm
WxDxH

Base Armature
15x15x60 cm

cm
WxDxH

WxDxH

#7
40x40x54

#11
38x34x55

#12
55x38x32

#14
59x43x43

#15
40x45x31

#17
46x39x17

42x42x63

#19
35x36x17

41x38x66

#23
40x42x57

#24
38x42x43

43 cm

#27
54x35x34

#28
46x40x57

#29
46x47x17

47 cm

53x40x63

#34
37x40x46

#34
42x39x43

Apollo #1/2
100x100x42 cm
WxDxH

Apollo #2/2
100x100x43

Venus #1/2
86x88x81
WxDxH

127x63x63
WxDxH

Dafne

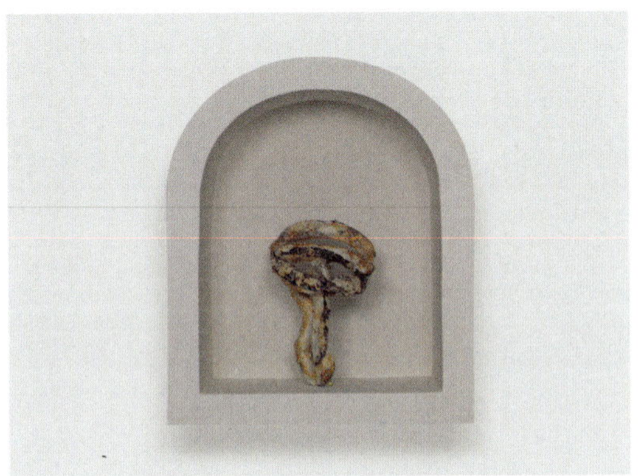

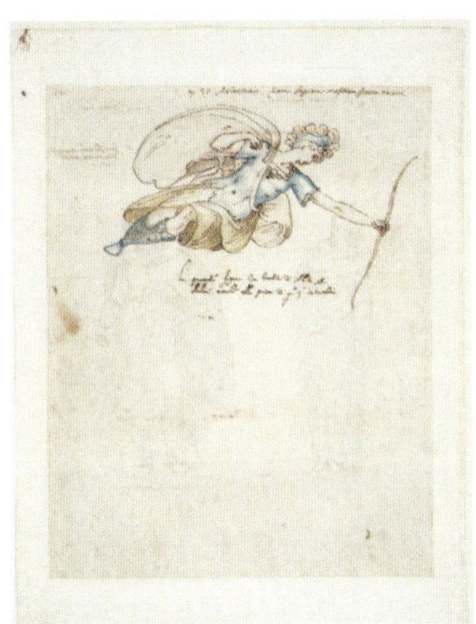

Apollo

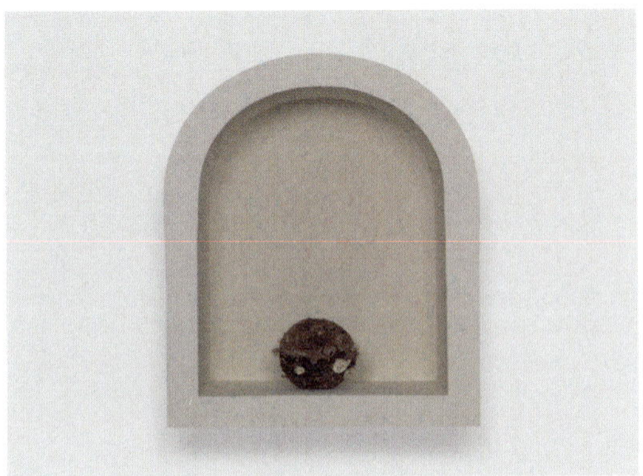

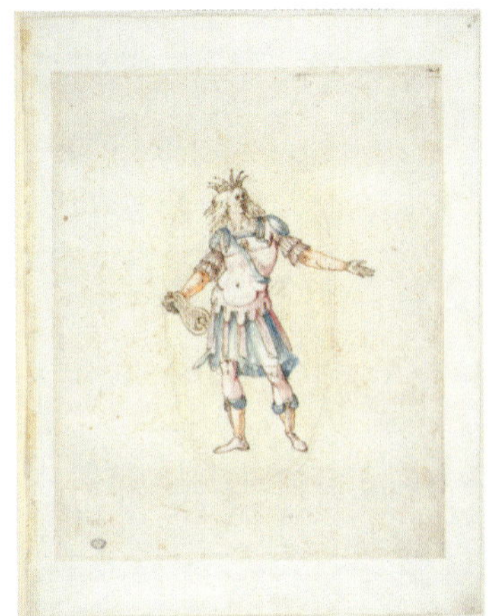

dafne phono libretto 1

Wherein the original Italian libretto of
Dafne is translated into Abkhaz,
San Juan Quiahije Eastern Chatino, Latin,
Spanish for Silbo Gomero, and !Xoon.

[Prologo]

Ovidio

Da' fortunati campi, ove immortali
godonsi a l'ombra de' frondosi mirti
i graditi del ciel felici spirti,
mostromi in questa notte a voi mortali.

Quel mi son io che su la dotta lira
cantai le fiamme de' celesti amanti
e i transformati lor vari sembianti
soave sì ch'il mondo anco m'ammira.

Indi l'arte insegnai come si deste
in un gelato cor fiamma d'Amore
e come in libertà ritorni un core
cui son d'Amor le fiamme aspre e moleste.

Seguendo or di giovar l'antico stile,
con chiaro esempio a dimostrarvi piglio
quanto sia, donne e cavalier', periglio
la potenza d'Amor recarsi a vile.

Vedrete lagrimar quel Dio ch'in cielo
porta in bel carro d'or la luce al giorno
e della amata ninfa il lume adorno
adorar dentro al trasformato stelo.

[Primo coro]

Coro. Eco.
Ebra di sangue in questo oscuro bosco
giacea pur dianzi la terribil fera. *Era.*
Dunque più non attosca
nostre belle contrade? altrove è gita? *Ita.*
Oimè! chi n'assicura
s'oggi tornar pur deve il mostro rio? *Io.*
Chi sei tu, che n'affidi e ne console? *Sole.*
Il Sol tu sei? tu sei di Delo il dio? *Io.*
Hai l'arco teco per ferirlo, Apollo? *Hollo.*

[Актәи ахор]

Ахор. (Аныҩбжьы.)
Абна еинчыла илаиан
ашьажәра иашьыз агыгшәыг ҿаасҭа.
Уаҳагьы изархәамгарыма
ҳқыҭа ԥшӡа? Цьара иқәтцны ицама?
Аха, ҳара ҳзыхьчода нас
уи аҿаасҭа бааԥс иахьа ихынҳәраны иҟазар?
Узусҭада уара, ҳгәы зырҭынчуа, ҳазҟажо? (*Амра!*)
Амра уоума уара? Делосаа рынцәахә уоума?

Nten^{B} ndla^{K}. (Ngya^{A} tyqi^{c}.)
Kqwi^{f} qo^{E} jlyo^{I} yta^{A} jne^{G} su^{G} neq^{c} shqo^{f} re^{c},
kwan^{H} niyan^{J} su^{G} neq^{A} chin^{I} janq^{G} ne^{c}. *(Su^{G} kanq^{H})*
Ne^{c} in^{H} ja^{A} la^{I} qa^{J} jla^{H} yweq^{H}
Neq^{c} kshinq^{c} no^{E} qnya^{E} ka^{J} niya^{K} qna^{G} a^{J} Jen^{c} ngya^{E} shka^{I} kchin^{I} a^{J}. *(Ngya^{A})*
Qna^{f} ka^{J} qne^{E} jlon^{H}on^{E}, ton^{G} nga^{J} no^{I} qne^{J} qna^{f} qna^{G} ne^{c}
si^{K} kla^{K} ton^{K} neq^{A} kchin^{I} janq^{G} ni^{c} kanq^{H} qa^{J}. *(Naq^{G})*
Ton^{G} nga^{J} qwen^{I} chaq^{E} no^{E} qne^{J} tlaq^{H} qwa^{G} in^{H}.

[Prologus]

Publius Ovidius Naso
Divum clara cohors foliis quam myrtus inumbrat
Manibus aucta piis coetus conducit amoenos:
Nuper ab Elysii qui promunt gaudia campis
Transitus his, vestras, perituri, prosequor aures
Cui numeros ut agam sapiens lyra coepta secundat
Qualis amor superum, quas mutent numina formas.
Sic meruit carmen, tantae dulcedinis ictus
Ut non desit adhuc vatis mihi claritas artis.
Sum qui olim docui sollertem vincere flammam
Viscera stricta gelu; sedari nec minus iram
Saevam qua subigit sibi corda ligata Cupido.
Nondum deficient priscae gestamina Musae
Donec erunt semper patienda pericula vobis,
O domini dominaeque meae, sub Amore tyranno,
Quae monstrare mihi debent spectabile casu
Ne temeretur atrox in mente potestas earum.
Vobis mira patent: lacrimis ut lumina nigrant
Cui renovare licet curru moderamina lucis
Semideaeque procus per cultus aurifer exstans
Vix accincta colat terreno pectora libro.

Coro. (Eco).
Ebria de sangre en este bosque oscuro
ahora yace la bestia terrible. *(Ahí estaba!)*
¿Para que no envenene
nuestro campo hermoso? ¿Se ha ido a otro lado?
(¡Ido!)
¡Ay de nosotros! ¿quién nos defenderá
si la bestia malvada volviera hoy? *(¡Yo!)*
¿Quién eres tú que nos da confianza y consuelo?
(¡El sol!)

ǂuka lâc ǂaan
Qxai N!aga ki nǂahnya ki
Ae qaye *(Ee qayi)*
Ee llaha lqhu si qlahan ka ǂhann
Ki si ke n’ore ke ǂai glahm ke? Ee ka ha sáà?
(Ee sáà)
Oh Ee ha-ke ka huiki
Siǂqhai ka tshari taam ki tshai qai (!) *(Nn n)*
Aa ke hake ke si ‘obe ki sai ke *(llahan)*
Aa ke llahan? Aa ki G’ohu Delos lai *(Nn n)*

S’hai l’arco tuo, saetta fin che mora
questo mostro crudel che ne divora. *Ora.*

Fitone e Apollo in scena.
Morto il Fitone.

[Primo quadro]

Apollo
Pur giacque estinto alfine
in sul terren sanguigno
da l’invitto arco mio l’angue maligno.
Securi itene al prato,
ninfe e pastor’, ite securi al bosco.
Non più di fiamm’ o tosco
infetta il chiaro ciel l’orribil fiato.
Tornin le belle rose
nelle guance amorose;
torni tranquillo il cor, sereno il volto.
Io l’alma e ’l fiato al crudo serpe ho tolto.

[Secondo coro]

Coro
Almo Dio, ch’il carro ardente
per lo ciel volgendo intorno
vesti il dì d’un aureo manto,
se tra l’ombre orride algente
splende il ciel di lumi adorno,
è pur tua la gloria e il vanto.
Se germoglian frondi e fiori,
selve e prati, e rinovella
l’ampia terra il suo bel manto,
se de’ suoi dolci tesori
ogni pianta si fa bella,
è pur tua la gloria e ’l vanto.

(*Сара!*)
Ахәымпал умоума узлахысуа, Аполлон?
(Исымоуп!)
Ахәымпал умазар, ишьы
ари ҳазфо аҵәыршәага бааҧсы *(Уажәыҵәҟьа!)*

[Аҩбатәи ахор]

Ахор
Зегь зымчу Анцәа ду,
амца зхылҵуа ауардын иақәтәаны ажәҩан иху,
ахьтәы мшьамбала ирҕьшӡа ҳамш.
Иҵааршәыроу агагақәа ирыбжьысны
ажәҩан лашарбагала ихҟьазар,
изыбзоуроу уара уоуп, ҳгәазырҳага лаша.
Абыҕьқәеи ашәҭқәеи пытуазар,
абнақәеи адәқәеи
адгьыл каршәрақәеи ирықәыршәу дырҿыцуазар;
иара аҵьуҳарла иарҕьшӡозар
ҵиаа цыҕхьаӡа,
ари зегь зыбзоуру уара уоуп, ҳгәазырҳага лаша.

(Qo^{c} kcha^{G})
Ta^{A} qwen^{A} nga^{G} qo^{c} kcha^{G} a^{J}. Ta^{A} qo^{c} Delos
nga^{G} a^{J} *(Naq^{G})*
Apolo, qo^{E} slaq^{H} qin^{G} chaq^{f} kjwi^{J} cha^{G} qin^{A}
a^{A} *(Qo^{E} ran^{f} qnya^{J})*
Si^{K} qo^{E} slaq^{H} qin^{G} in^{H}, yjwi^{I} sqen^{I} la^{G} qin^{A}
neq^{A} chin^{I} re^{c} kyqan^{J} qa^{E} no^{A} tqi^{I} qne^{I} qo^{E}on^{E}.
(Qa^{K} ne^{K})

Nten^{B} ndla^{K}
Qo^{c} nlo^{I}, no^{A} nsqwi^{A} neq^{c} tykwan^{f} sha^{f}
ntykwi^{H} ntyjin^{B} ngya^{K} tu^{c}-kwan^{c},
nqne^{J} tykanq^{c} tsan^{A} qo^{E} ska^{J} teq^{A} sha^{f}.
Ja^{A} no^{A} ndiya^{c} shi^{E}, ntqo^{E} tkwi^{c} sha^{f} tlaq^{B} keq^{K}
ndwi^{E} sha^{f} niya^{K} tu^{K} tkwan^{c},
qwen^{A} nga^{J} no^{A} nlo^{I} la^{J} ti^{J}.
Qan^{E} an^{E} nkaq^{A} qo^{E} ke^{c} ndwa^{B} yten^{K} ran^{f}
qo^{E} neq^{c} shqo^{f} qo^{E} neq^{c} shinq^{c}, qo^{E}
qo^{E} yu^{A} qne^{J} kwi^{E} na^{f} ntyqya^{J} chonq^{G} in^{H}; nda^{H} ska^{G}
ran^{f} qo^{E} na^{f} sqwe^{f} qin^{J} ran^{f} in^{H}
qo^{E} nda^{H} ska^{G} yka^{A} ke^{c} qne^{J} tykanq^{c} qin^{E}
qwen^{A} nga^{J} no^{A} nlo^{I} la^{J} ti^{J}.

¿Eres el Sol? ¿Eres el dios de Delos? (*¡Yo!*)
¿Llevas el arco contigo para herirlo, Apolo?
(*¡Lo tengo!*)
Si tienes tu arco, dispara a muerte
a este monstruo cruel que nos devora. (*¡Ahora!*)

Aa ǂaha ka tahba? (Apollo) Nn ǂaha
Aa ǂaha ka tahba Nǂoha qaye
Sinlohan ka kaan aan luri. *(Nlahi)*

Coro
Dios divino, quien en tu carruaje de fuego
paseas alrededor de todo el cielo,
vistes el día de un manto dorado.
Si entre la horrorosa sombra helada
el cielo brilla con tu luz,
tuyos también son la gloria y la jactancia.
Si brotan frondas y flores,
Bosques y prados, y
la tierra entera renueva su hermoso manto; si con
sus dulces tesoros,
todas las plantas embellecen
tuyos también son la gloria y la jactancia.

Nǂum se laa ǂaan
Aa ki Gluhu ki si
N!ari kii
Ee si qain N!ore
Som hanti ka llahong
N!ori ǂae llang ǂae N!ahin sae
Aa lai N!ari saar si si GʘOohm kaan
Nǂahmi ii ka si qára
NʘOaha saa na ki tuu qayan
NʘOahan ka si qain ka tam ke
Ao G!uhu ki G!ahin kii
Tahng Mahoeko koon si nlaar laon ka si G'xaru
Ki G!uhu !uni

Per te vive e per te gode
quanto scerne occhio mortale,
o rettor del carro eterno;
ma si lassi ogn'altra lode,
sol de l'arco e dello strale
voli il grido al ciel superno.
Nobil vanto: il fier dragone
di velen, di fiamm' armato,
sul terren versat'ha l'alma.
Per trecciar fregi e corone
al ben crin di raggi ornato
qual fia degno o lauro o palma?

[Secondo quadro]

Amore e Venere

Amore
Che tu vadi cercando o giglio o rosa
per infiorart'il crine,
non ti vo' creder, no, madre vezzosa.

Venere
Che cerco dunque, o figlio?

Amore
Rosa non già né giglio.
Cerchi d'Adone o d'altro via più bello
leggiadro pastorello.

Venere
Ah tristo, tristo! Ecco il signor di Delo.
Pe' boschi oggi sen van gli dèi del cielo.

О, ҧсра зқәым ауардын ныҟәызцо уара,
убзоуралоуп аҧсы злаҭоу иагьзлагәырҕьо аҧсра алакҭа. Аҽхәаҧхьызқәа зегьы наскьаганы,
ахыци ахәымпали мацароуп ишьҭыхтәу
аҳәҳәабжь ажәҩанахь ианҩеиуа.
Иҳаракӡоу аҽхәаҧхьыз!
Ашҳами амцабзи рыла еиқәныху агәылшьап ҧагьа аҧсы ныҭшәан адгьыл иныкәҳаи.
Агәыргьынқәа ҧатәуп
Амырхәага здыҷҷало алахь ҧшӡазы
иаҳа ианааларызи уи: адаҧа ма апальма бҕьы иалху акәу?

[Аҩбатәи асцена]

Амури Венереи

Амур
Азышәҭыш акәу агәил акәу бзышьҭоу
быхцәы злабырҧшӡо?
Сан бзиа, быгәра сызгаӡом

Венера
Сзышьҭаларызи нас, сычкәын?

Амур
Агәилгьы акәым азышәҭышгьы акәым,
бара бзышьҭоу Адонис иоуп ма иаҳа иҧшӡоу
иблахкыгоу хьчаҩык

Венера
О, арыцҳара, арыцҳара! Абар дахьыҟоу Делос аиҳабы: иахьа абна илсны ицоит анцәахәқәа зегьы.

Qwen^{A} stu^{K} qin^{G} yla^{G} sha^{f} liyu^{I} re^{c}
ndiya^{A} na^{f} lo^{E} qin^{J} sqyu^{c} ke^{A} lo^{A} qo^{c}
qo^{c} no^{E} nlo^{J} jnya^{f} sa^{A} tykwi^{E}
Ndiya^{A} no^{A} ja^{A} la^{I} nga^{J} chaq^{f} qo^{E} ntqen^{A} chaq^{f} tyqo^{H} ran^{f};
la^{E} yka^{A} qo^{E} ke^{A} no^{A} nlyaq^{A} renq^{A} qo^{E} slaq^{H} ti^{J} janq^{G}
ntqen^{A} chaq^{f} jne^{J} chaq^{f} qo^{c} qna^{G} ti^{H} lo^{J} la^{E} tu^{c}-kwan^{c}.
Chaq^{f} qo^{c} no^{E} nyi^{A} ndwa^{B} ti^{K}. Qne^{A} jno^{A} no^{A} nlo^{J} kiq^{K},
ja^{A} no^{K} nshon^{H} nlyaq^{A} yan^{G} qo^{E} kiq^{A},
slu^{B} tyqi^{c} lo^{E} sha^{f} liyu^{I}.
Chaq^{f} shkwan^{B} kte^{K} lo^{A} ti^{f} qo^{K} na^{f} ndwa^{B} ke^{G}
chaq^{f} tykwa^{B} tqwa^{A} tykan^{G} no^{A} ndwi^{E} sha^{f} ndwi^{H}
ton^{G} nga^{J} no^{I} nlo^{I} la^{E}: ke^{c} ktanq^{B} qo^{E} ta^{A} tyjnya^{A}.

Skno^{K} qo^{E} jla^{A} sen^{I}

Skono^{K}
Ya^{A} soq^{c} la^{E} ke^{c} shlya^{E} qo^{E} ta^{A} ke^{c} jlyaq^{E}
chaq^{f} ka^{J} tykanq^{c} ke^{I}
Ja^{A} la^{I} ngya^{A} ntyqan^{A} renq^{H} qin^{G}, ja^{A} la^{I} ran^{f}, ma^{H} tya^{A},

Skono^{K}
Ni^{A} ke^{c} shlya^{E} ni^{A} ke^{c} jlyaq^{E}:
ntqan^{I} na^{G} qin^{A} Adonis qo^{E} ta^{A} shka^{I} no^{A} kyqyu^{E} ntyqya^{B} la^{K} niyan^{K}
qan^{K} ska^{K} keru^{B} no^{A} ndiya^{J} ndywiq^{I}.

Skono^{K}
Ni^{A} sya^{H} qne^{A} jno^{A} no^{A} nlo^{J} kiq^{K}
ja^{A} la^{I} nkjwi^{G} qo^{E} slaq^{H} qnya^{J},
sqwe^{f} qne^{H} kta^{f} ja^{A} la^{I} ta^{H} ndiyeq^{f} riq^{c} qnya^{J},
qo^{E} naq^{G}, Apolo, naq^{G} ngan^{J} qo^{c} qin^{E} tu^{c}-kwan^{c}

A través de ti vive y goza
todo lo que percibe el ojo mortal,
oh gobernante del carruaje eterno.
No obstante todos los elogios deberían dejarse a lado;
más el del arco y la flecha
si es que el grito se eleva a los cielos más altos.
¡Noble gloria! El dragón honrado,
armado de veneno y llamas,
ha vertido su alma sobre la tierra.
Para trenzar guirnaldas y coronas
en la frente hermosa engalanada de rayos,
¿Cuál será más digno, el laurel o la palma?

Cupido y Venus

Cupido
Que tú vayas buscando lirios o rosas
para adornar tu cabello
no lo quiero creer, no, hermosa Madre.

Venus
¿Entonces qué busco, hijo?

Cupido
Ni rosa, ni lirio:
busca a Adonis, u otro aún más hermoso y
encantador pastor.

Venus
Oh, vaya, ¡vaya! Aquí está el señor de Delos:
hoy todos los dioses del cielo pasan por los bosques.

O G!uhu ki nǂahan ka lái
Xaxa Llu aa juru ke lahin nn !ahang
Siisi Glohong tahbo jaa qXaan
Oh Nllahri ii jahin GΘoqhm
Ii Nǂuhmi ki taom ki taan jáàn
Ii Si tshuum ǂaqi laa tshuum saa
ke N!ore sa-an
Ee si qain-qain
Ki lhou-lhausi
Θahi haka ki qaha ki taam? Gllaha
lae lloa

Cupid |ai Venus

Cupid
Aa si sii !ahang blumke n|ai ‘n|ahang ka nlang
Nn ||’oa sai ǂumka, Nn Aqe ke qain ke

Venus
Aa ǂaha si nǂain n|ang nn ki sai g!ahang tahi nn Θaa

Cupid
Aa |hoa si !ahang blomke,
Aa si !ahi Adonis oǂ g!hang, gain
kee l’aan g!ahan

Venus
Oh Nn Nǂaho Nǂaho, G!huu ki kái Delos
Tshai kai ki G!huu lai N’ori ii ka |hoa ka nΘahan !”aan

Apollo, Amore e Venere

Apollo
Dimmi, possente arciero,
qual fiera attendi o qual serpente al varco,
ch'hai la faretra e l'arco?

Amore
Se di questo arco mio
non fu Fitone ucciso,
arcier non son però degno di riso,
ma son del ciel, Apollo, un nume anch'io.

Apollo
Sollo. Ma quando scocchi
l'arco, sbendi tu gli occhi
o ferisci all'oscuro, arciero esperto?

Amore
Sì, lo saprai per certo!

Apollo
Ah, tu t'adiri a torto.
O mi perdona, Amore,
se mi vuoi ferir, risparmia il core.

Amore
So ben che non paventi
la forza d'un fanciullo,
saettator di mostri e di serpenti.
Ma prendi pur di me gioco e trastullo!

Venere
Vedrai che grave rischio è scherzar seco,
benché sia pargoletto, ignudo e cieco.

Амур
Агәылшьап сара схы иамшьызаргьы,
сара иатәарымбо хысҩым,
сара соуп, Аполлон, ажәҩан анцәахәы.

Амур
Ааи, уара ари, хымҕада, еилукаартә уҟоуп!

Амур
Хәыҷык имч ушацәымшәо здыруеит,
о, агыгшәыг ҿаасҭақәеи амаҭқәеи зшьуа,
уажә сара усхыччоит, усылахәмаруеит.

Венера
Иубара уҟоуп закә шәарҭароу иаҵоу уи
илахәмарра,
иагьа дыҕшқазаргьы, дҟьантазны
длашәызаргьы.

Skono^{K}
Kwiq^{J} ran^{f}, ntyqan^{G} ka^{J} ru^{K} ntyqan^{I}.

Skono^{K}
Jlyo^{H} sqwe^{f} renq^{H} chaq^{f} ja^{A} la^{I} ntsen^{G}
weza^{K} qin^{K} no^{A} shwe^{I},
nga^{G} ska^{A} neq^{A} shqan^{K} no^{A} ntjwi^{J} neq^{A} chin^{I}
qo^{E} jna^{E},
ja^{A} ndyi^{I} chaq^{f} ndiyeq^{f} riq^{E} qo^{E} shtyi^{H} qo^{G} qnya^{A}.

Apollo, Cupido y Venus

Cupido
Incluso si el dragón
no fue muerto por mi arco,
no soy arquero que aún merezca desprecio,
pero también yo, Apolo, soy un dios de los cielos.

Cupido
¡Sí, lo sabrás con certeza!

Cupido
Sé bien que no tienes miedo
de la fuerza de un niño
oh, asesino de monstruos y serpientes,
más, te burlas de mí y te divierte.

Coro
El que viva desencadenado de los lazos de amor,
que goce felizmente de su libertad,
pero no soberbio: envuelto en una nube oscura
para nosotros es el alto decreto del cielo.
Si ahora no sientes ni poco ni mucho Amor,
mañana tendrás un corazón perturbado e inquieto,
y hallarás que dueño cruel y severo
es el Amor, que antes tu despreciaste tan altivo.

Apollo |ai Cupid, Venus

Cupid
Nn ku ka xabe ||hoa qanya |xhuun
l''aan thaba
Nn ||hoa ka n|ohasa aqa thaba, xata nn
Ki Apollo nn xare ke ki G!huu

Cupid
Eeh Aa ke 'n|ahi |'om n|ang ki ka nǂoha
Sa aga

Cupid
Nn l''om n|ang aa ki si nǂung kaan lae
sil''oase n|aa kaan ke Θage kee.
Oh Nn
|''om n|aa ki ka qaisa aqa |xhuun
|aan si gǂxore |aan
Nn |''om n|aa ki ka qaisa aqa, Só-
aan ka tana khuni-
khoan ka khang

Venus
Aa ka n|ang ka haa n||agha n|aa
ke ka n||ahama kaa kaan Ee xabe ke Θgage nn
l''oaka Nn ||ama ke !uni

[Terzo coro]

Coro.
Chi da' lacci d'Amor vive disciolto
della sua libertà goda pur lieto,
superbo no: d'oscura nube involto
stassi per noi del Ciel l'alto decreto.
S'or non senti d'Amor poco né molto,
avrai dimane il cor turbato e 'nquieto,
e signor proverai crudo e severo
Amor che dianzi disprezasti altiero.

[Ахҧатәи ахор]

Ахор
Абзиабара зҽазымҭакәа иҟоу
ихақәитра деигәырӷьалааит,
аха рацәак иҽеимырҧагьакәа: аҧҭа еиқәаара иҽылахәаны
хыхьынтә ишаҳдырбаз аҧҟара дуӡӡа ала
Маҷк иадамхаргьы абзиабара умамзар,
уаҵәы агәҭынчымра уоуеит,
насгьы уи абзиабара уара узы агәыцьбареи
рыцҳашьара злами аҧшәымахоит,
ахаангьы иуаҭәаумшьоз.

nten^{B} ndla^{K}
No^{A} ndon^{G} riq^{c} ndwa^{B} ska^{K} ti^{J} sha^{f} liyu^{I}
nda^{f} la^{J} wan^{J} chaq^{f} tyqan^{J} ndon^{G} riq^{c} ska^{E} ti^{J},
ja^{A} la^{I} qne^{J} ndiyeq^{f} riq^{c}: ntykonq^{J} yqwi^{I} neq^{c} ska^{E} ko^{G} tla^{B}
nga^{J} ran^{f} jnya^{f} ntqo^{E} tu^{c}-kwan^{c} la^{E} ti^{J} qin^{J} wa^{G} re^{c}.
ne^{c} in^{H} shqnyi^{A} qa^{J} nga^{J} qin^{G}
kya^{H} la^{E} tyqan^{A} yqwi^{A} ti^{A} sya^{K} qin^{G} nga^{J}
tyqan^{G} chaq^{f} nga^{G} ska^{A} shqna^{K} shqan^{K} qo^{E} tji^{A}
chaq^{f} sqwe^{f}, no^{A} nda^{f} ndiyeq^{f} riq^{E} ti^{E} sqne^{E}.

[Terzo quadro]

Dafne. Apollo. Amore.

Dafne
Del fugitivo cervo
quest'è pur orma impressa:
fusse almen qui vicin la fera stessa.

Apollo
Qual d'un bel ciglio adorno
spira lume gentil ch'al cor mi giunge?
Bella ninfa gentil, che miri intorno?

Dafne
Guardo se qualche belva
errasse dentro a questa oscura selva.

Apollo
Senza che dardo avventi o l'arco scocchi,
valle cercando o monti,

[Ахҧатәи асцена]

Дафне, Аполлон, Амур

Дафне
Абри ашьҭа,
ибналаз абынҽеацә иатәуп:
иара ашәарах ахаҭа ааигәа иҟандаз.

Дафне
Ари абна лашьца бынҽеацәк
ылазмашь ҳәа сыҧшуеит

Дафне
Абна илоу агыгшәыгкәеи абнақәеи рыда
даҽа гәахәарак сыздырӡом; насгьы зымҩа иацәҟьалаз шьабстаки
ибжьасу абынҳәеи сызшьыр, уи аасҭа еиҳау гәахәара сымаӡам.

Dafne, Apolo qo^{E} Skono^{K}

Dafne
No^{A} qin^{A} jnyaq^{E} no^{A} ntqan^{I} sna^{f}
kwi^{J} la^{E} no^{A} nde^{c} nga^{J} jyaq^{f} slaq^{J}:
si^{K} no^{K} ntqan^{I} chinq^{H} neq^{A} chin^{I} janq^{G} qin^{K} ti^{H} re^{c}.

Dafne
Ni^{E} qyan^{H} si^{K} ntqen^{G} neq^{I} chin^{I}
ntqan^{I} ntqan^{A} neq^{c} shqo^{f} tla^{B} re^{K}.

Dafne
Ja^{A} la^{I} ndiya^{J} renq^{H} shka^{I} qne^{A}, ni^{A} shka^{I} na^{f} shonq^{B}
qne^{A} jla^{f} qo^{E} neq^{c} yka^{K} ti^{J}; siyenq^{f} qan^{H} qo^{E} ndon^{G} qa^{J} renq^{H}
si^{K} kon^{L} qin^{E} jnyaq^{E} no^{A} ntqan^{I} sna^{f} qo^{E} ta^{A} kon^{L} qin^{K} kweq^{G} shinq^{c}.

Llahise laa ǂaam
Ee ||ahan ||hoa siΘqxohm ke
|uhung ke ee !óè ke siΘqxobe
Xata ee |hoa nǂung n|ae ki
kaa kaan Ee xabe ke Θgage nn l''oaka
Nn ||ama ke !uni
khom|ae: Ee |ahan n||aga
G!uhu kaò si N!uni ka kcchang ki
ǂau ki kahan kaan
Aa n|ahi ||ama ki |agm ke aa kaa ||ama kii
Khobe aa |ahan ki N!ahi xaba
|aham ee ka khaoxa, |ahom ii ka ǂahni lai
Ke Ii ki ǂaha

Dafne, Apollo y Cupido

Dafne
Del venado fugitivo
esta es la misma huella impresa:
si tan solo la bestia misma estuviera
aquí cerca.

Dafne
Estoy buscando si alguna bestia
anda vagando en este bosque oscuro.

Dafne
No codicio otra presa, otro deleite
más que las fieras y los bosques; y
estoy contenta y alegre
disparándole a una cierva errante o a
un jabalí salvaje.

Defne |ai Apollo, Cupid

Defne
||oa nǂang kaan aa !ahang |oan ka Ee sa ku
||aa !ahang |ai

Defne
Nn si !ahang 'N!ohqan nn ǂhaa ||hoa |o n|ang
ka n||qba saa ke

Defne
Nn ||hoa si n!uni ki ǂxam |qhai ki si qaiyi tam
thong |qhong kuru ica tam
||hoa |ang qanya NΘahan xata nn |''aan ku gΘxhum
Nn qaiye khari ke

far nobil preda p‹u›oi co’ tuoi begl’occhi.
Dafne
Altra preda non bramo, altro diletto
che fere e selve, e son contenta e lieta
se damm’ errante o fier cignal saetto.

Apollo
Anch’io so tender l’arco,
e quando non ti spiaccia,
farem d’accordo dilettosa caccia.

Dafne
Altro che ’l dardo mio
non vo’ compagno; a dio.

Apollo
Oimè, non tanta fretta:
aspetta, ninfa, aspetta.

Amore
Ve’ che ti giunsi al varco.
O impara a disprezzar l’etate e l’arco!

[Quarto coro]

Coro.
Qual nuova meraviglia
vedut’han gl’occhi miei: selvaggia fronda
farsi la chioma bionda,
e ’l piè, ch’or or fuggia veloce e sciolto,
per entro il suol sepolto
germogliar rami e foglie.
Forse alle caste voglie
la sacra Dea, poscia ch’indarno è ’l corso,
cotal porge soccorso,
né per castigo no, ma per pietade

Дафне
Схыц ада
даҽеа ҩызак дысҭахӡам; абзиараз.

Амур
Ацәҟьа ушасыркыз убома.
О, сықәра атәамбареи ахырхәареи закәу
удыруазааит!

[Аҧшьбатәи ахор]

Ахор
Закә ссирузеи иҿыцны
ирбо сыблақәа!
Ахцәхыш аҵламахәқәа иреиҧшхеит,
уажә аҧхьа ирласны иҩуаз ашьапы
амахәқәеи абыӷьқәеи адгьыл
иҵацаланы иакәаҳаит.
Иҟалап, иҧшьоу анцәахәы (Диана)
агәахәтәы цқьа ҭакс иалҭаз – абналара шбашоу
анеилкааха ас еиҧш иҟоу ацхыраара
аӡәы иҭархаразы акәымкәа, агәыҳалалразы ауп
иблахкыгоу аҧсы ашәаҧыџьаҧ ахь изиалгаз.

Dafne
qo^{E} slaq^{H} ti^{J} re^{c} qnya^{E},
ja^{A} la^{I} qne^{J} chaq^{f} shka^{I} la^{J} nten^{B} tsa^{K} qon^{E}; sqan^{J}
lan^{H}.

Skono^{K}
Wa^{c} ntqan^{I} ne^{c} a^{E}, ndiyu^{E} neq^{c} sqo^{E}.
Na^{L}, wa^{c} ntqan^{I} na^{f} ndiya^{E} chaq^{f} nda^{H} ndiyeq^{f} riq^{c}
neq^{J} jla^{J} qo^{E} slaq^{H} qin^{J} a^{J}.

nten^{B} ndla^{K}
Tyu^{H} u^{J} ntyqya^{J} qa^{E} niya^{J} re^{c}
ntqan^{G} sqyu^{c} ke^{A} lon^{H} re^{c}, neq^{c} nkaq^{E} yka^{J} nkqa^{G}
ndwi^{E} kchanq^{G} ksi^{B} ke^{G}.
qo^{E} lo^{A} qen^{G} ti^{A} ndwi^{E} kyaq^{J} sna^{f} jen^{c} ngya^{E}
ntyjyuq^{E} neq^{c} yu^{A}
ntsu^{I} yten^{J} na^{f} jnyi^{J} qo^{E} nkaq^{A}…
Chin^{A} chaq^{f} la^{K} kwan^{H} ti^{J} niya^{J} shkwen^{B} chaq^{f} ndiye^{I}
ndwa^{B} ska^{K} ti^{J}
no^{H} nga^{J} qo^{c} [Diana]—kwi^{J} qo^{H} qa^{J} sna^{f} ran^{f}—
nda^{f} yaq^{c} qin^{E},
sqi^{E} chaq^{f} kyqya^{A}, sqi^{E} ran^{f}, nga^{J} ran^{f} chaq^{f} qna^{f} riq^{c},

Dafne
Aparte de mi flecha,
no quiero compañía; Hasta siempre.

Defne
Nn |"aan ka thabe nn ||hoa si g!abor
N|hoo, g!ahi sai |ai

Cupid
Ha sii n|aam nn a han |oake
Oh ||xaa-||xaa ka tam n|aa ka si nǂuhi ka
|ao kurike |aan kaa thaba

Coro
Que nueva maravilla
mis ojos han visto! En frondas que parecen árboles
el pelo rubio se ha vuelto,
y el pie que acaba de correr rápido y libre,
enterrado en el suelo,
brotando ramas y hojas..
Tal vez en respuesta a los límpidos deseos
la diosa sagrada [Diana]—ya que huir fue en vano—
ofreció tal ayuda,
no como castigo, no, sino por misericordia

Haka se laa ǂaan
Thai n||oqhang ka gain ka
Kng na ka nlaan |aan !oni!
G||aha ee tshare tam nn sa-an |ohong ka G!agni kaan
Ee nǂuhung ka n|ahi si ||agba
Aa koekà qaru
Nn se nǂubisike |ai nǂahmi
Ee qai |ae si N!uhi ke kuru ta n||ahba qae ke
Ee ||ahmtu (Diona)
||u |oe si!ose n|ae ee !au N||ohung
Nn ||hoa ki |ahbi, ha-aan nn ki g|uqung
Xata ee |aa tshuumsa ka gain ka a dái nΘhai

cangia in nuovo arbuscel l'alma beltade.
[Quarto quadro]

Apollo
Dunque ruvida scorza
chiuderà sempre la beltà celeste?
Lumi, voi che vedeste
l'alta beltà ch'a lagrimar vi sforza,
affisatevi pure in questa fronde:
qui posa e qui s'asconde
il mio ben, il mio core, il mio tesoro,
per cui, bench'immortal, languisco e moro.
Ninfa sdegnosa e schiva
che fuggendo l'amor d'un dio del cielo,
cangiasti in verde lauro il tuo bel velo,
non fia però ch'io non t'adori ed ami,
ma sempre al mio crin d'auro
faran g‹h›irlanda le tue fronde e I rami.
Ma deh, se in questa fronde
senti il mio pianto, odi la nobil cetra
quai doni a te dal ciel cantando impetra.
Non curi la mia pianta o fiamma o gelo,
sien di vivo smeraldo eterni i pregi,
né l'offenda già mai l'ira del cielo.
I bei cigni di Dirce e i sommi regi
de' verdeggianti rami al crin famoso
portin segno d'onor ghirlande e fregi.
Gregge mai né pastor fia che noioso
del verde manto tuo ti spoglie e prive,
alla grat'ombra il dì liet'e gioioso
tragg‹h›in liete cantando e ninfe e dive.

shqan^{E} tyqi^{c} lwi^{f} qo^{E} shka^{I} shinq^{c} nkqa^{G} a^{J}.

ella cambió a un alma tan hermosa a un arbusto.

[Quinto coro]

Coro
Bella ninfa fugitiva,
sciolt'e priva
del mortal tuo nobil velo,
godi pur pianta novella,
casta e bella,
cara al mondo e cara al cielo.
Tu non curi nembi o tuoni,
tu coroni
cigni, regi e dèi celesti;
geli il ciel o infiamm' e scaldi,
di smeraldi
lieta ognor t'adorni e vesti.
Godi pur de' doni egregi;
i tuo' pregi
non invidio e non desio.
Io, se mai d'Amor m'assale
aureo strale,
non vo' guerra con un dio.
S'a fuggir muovo le piante
vero amante,
contr'Amor cruda e superba,
venir possa il mio crin d'aureo
non pur laureo,
ma qual è più miser' erba.
Sia vil canna il mio crin biondo
ch‹e› l'immondo
gregge ognor schiante e dirame,
sia vil fien ch'a' crudi denti
degl'armenti
tragga ognor l'avida fame.
Ma s'a' preghi sospirosi,
amorosi,
di pietà sfavillo ed ardo,

[Ахәбатәи ахор]

Ахор
Иҩны ицо анимфа ԥшӡа,
иԥсыша аформа ԥшӡа иацәцаз,
бгәырҕьала,
аӡәгьы дызкьымсыз атцла ҿа,
дгьыли жәҩани ирзеиԥшу.
Адыд мацәыси ақәыршҩы аазго аԥҭақәеи шәрыцәшәаӡом шәара,
раҳра рышәҭоит
аӡыԥҟақәеи аҳцәеи жәҩантә анцәахәқәеи;
ажәҩан итцааршәым, ма уарԥхо аҟара амца акыма,
ианакәзаалакь шәгәырҕьатцәа шәыҿшәырԥшӡоит маҭәа ԥшӡалеи,
хаҳә иатцәалеи.
Шәеигәырҕьала ишәымоу
шәыпату,
сара сызтцамшьыцуа сзышьҭам.
Избанзар, мышкызны абзиабара ахыц сықәшәаргьы
нцәахәык сиабашьуам.
Абзиабара цәымҕны, рыцҳашьарак сзымдыруа,
бзиа сызбатцәҟьо
сицәцарц азы сшьапы еихызгар,
сыхьтәы хцәы
адаԥабҕьы еиԥш акәымкәа,
аҳаскьын атиаа иаҩызахаait.
Сыхцәы лаша, игәыҳәны иҟоу араҳә ирфаз,
насгьы иԥсаҟьаны икарԥсаз,
илаҟәу амахәқәа ирҩызахаait,
амла бааԥсы иархагаз,
угәы ҭызҟьо ахаԥыц бааԥсқәа змоу агыгшәыгқәа
рыраҳә згәыдлаз аҭәаҟәа лаҟәы иаҩызахаait.

nten^{B} ndla^{K}

nten^{B} ndla^{K}
Ntyqya^{J} sqen^{G}, she^{c} ntqan^{I} ntyqwi^{I} ktsiq^{f},
la^{G} renq^{f} qo^{E} kwi^{E} qo^{H} renq^{J} qin^{J}
sqwe^{f} sya^{K} qin^{G}, chaq^{f} nga^{G} nten^{B},
yka^{A} kwi^{B}, yka^{A} jneq^{E} ndon^{G} ti^{J} riq^{E},
kwiq^{c} no^{E} jneq^{E} nga^{J} qwen^{I}, no^{A} lwi^{f},
chonq^{G} ndiya^{J} riq^{c} sha^{E} liyu^{I} qo^{E} tu^{c} kwan^{c}.
ja^{A} la^{I} kwe^{A} tiq^{E} chaq^{f} ndwi^{E} ko^{G} tla^{B} qo^{E} tyqyu^{f};
tykwan^{f} ndwa^{B} ke^{I}
knyi^{c} ngoq^{c}, qo^{c} re^{B}, qo^{E} qo^{c} sten^{J}-en^{I};
si^{K} no^{K} ntyka^{c} keq^{c}, qo^{E} ta^{A} tyi^{H} tson^{B} tu^{c}-kwan^{c} qo^{E} kiq^{I},
qo^{E} ke^{A} nkqa^{G} sqwe^{f}
ndiya^{A} tsan^{A} ndon^{G} qa^{J} riq^{E} ntyku^{H} sqwe^{f} steq^{G} qo^{E} ntqne^{J} tykanq^{E} qin^{G} a^{J}.
Nda^{G} la^{J} stu^{K} qin^{G} qo^{E} ndiya^{A} na^{f};
qo^{E} weza^{K} ndiya^{I} qin^{G}
ja^{A} la^{I} ndiya^{J} renq^{H} qo^{E} ni^{A} ja^{A} la^{I} shkeq^{H} qnya^{J} qo^{E} kwa^{E}.
Tiyan^{J} ska^{I} tsan^{I} shkwi^{H} renq^{H} ska^{A} nten^{B}
slaq^{H} sha^{f},
ja^{A} la^{I} sqan^{J} son^{f} qo^{E} qo^{c} shqna^{K} an^{K}.
Si^{K} shnya^{K} ton^{G} kyanq^{A} chaq^{f} shna^{L} qin^{E}
ska^{A} nten^{B} no^{K} ndiya^{J} nyi^{I} riq^{c} qnya^{E},
shqan^{K} qo^{E} jno^{A} qne^{H} qnya^{J} chonq^{G} chaq^{f} ndiya^{J} renq^{H}
ktsi^{B} ntyka^{K} kchan^{G} kin^{J}
ja^{A} la^{I} ntyka^{c} ran^{f} ke^{c} ktanq^{B}
chonq^{G}, sqwe^{f} la^{J} ti^{J} si^{K} ntyka^{K} ran^{f} shinq^{c} tqi^{B}.
Chin^{A} chaq^{f} kchan^{G} ktsi^{B} kin^{J} ntyka^{c} ran^{f} kyaq^{J} yka^{A} tlaq^{B}
chaq^{f} qne^{A} tkonq^{E}
ndiya^{A} qne^{A} ntsa^{J} tqa^{G} qo^{E} nla^{H} yaq^{c} tqa^{G},
nda^{G} la^{J} chaq^{f} ka^{J} ki^{c} tiyu^{f} qin^{A} ke^{A} lqya^{A}

Coro
Hermosa ninfa fugitiva,
liberada y despojada
de tu noble forma mortal,
Alégrate, joven árbol,
casta y hermosa,
querida por el mundo y querida por el cielo.
No te preocupas por las nubes de tormenta o los truenos;
tú coronas
cisnes, reyes y dioses celestes;
si el cielo se congela, o se enciende en llamas y calienta,
con esmeraldas
adornate y vistete feliz siempre.
Goza de tus distinciones;
tus virtudes
que no envidio ni deseo.
Porque si alguna vez me sorprende el Amor
con su flecha dorada,
No peleare con un dios.
Que mi cabello rubio se convierta en humildes tallos
que el voraz
rebaño siempre destroce y desparrame,
que sea humilde heno, al que los brutales dientes
de rebaños
atraiga siempre
el hambre codiciosa.
Pero si al responder a un suspiro,
y súplicas amorosas,
resplandezco y ardo con piedad,
si prometo el sufrimiento ajeno
dulce esperanza

Korose |aa ǂaan
Silagan ke gain ke ee si |agba
Ee si qára nn ||hoa |ai ||ai ki ǂóóki
Ke |ae ǂaa ka sa ee ǂaha q|huu ǂae si N||ause
Ha | ééan gΘxohm
Aa |ae siqaye ǂaa |qahba
N!ore sa’an |qamka |ai N!ahri xare ke
Aa ||haa si |ae ke M’arase |ae G!oe ||qxana
Ee si ||ahang ke g!xára ke qainke N|ai ||xahi |qahan
Sid áo, Khoaxa |ai N!ari |ai G!huu
||hoa ||áè |ai N!ari sa-aan ka ||áan ke laé si||huu se
|áan |”omte ka ku ǂqahnaka
Aa |”aan kuri-kuri sigΘohm |ááka si sáé siqaye
g’áha |ae sigΘohm
|áa N|qaha ka qain ka
Nn ||hoe si shuuri |áá ka ǂa|ong ka si khang kaa
Aa ka xabe Nǂoha kaan laa |ahba ka siǂaqba kaan
Nn ||hoa si Nǂohma |ai G!huu
Nn ka ||hoa ||qaba kaan |ar |qahm
Nn |”aan ka si ||ára ko ku ||!oa ǂóaku |ae |qahm
Nn n|ang silhuuni ka si nǂaqba kaan
Nn n|ang s|huuni aa kai-na
Xata, ao K”oe g!obe ke ka ||”anya ke
L”ohong ka ||’aisa kaa
Ee aa !oa |”aa ki G!haru
Na kau Marike ka sin||aru ka siǂani kaan
Ee |”aa ki g!ahru kan,
tahang ka qai
N||ang aansa ka
Ee |” aa tshuu
Nn |ai |qahm toxoba
Nn NΘahan si Khuri nn, |”aan !gahn |ai |quhung
Nn si ǂhum |’ang ka

s'io prometto all'altrui pene
dolce spene
con un riso e con un sguardo,
non soffrir, cortese Amore,
ch'il mio ardore
prenda a scherno alma gelata,
non soffrir ch'in piaggia o in lido
core infido
m'abbandoni innamorata.
Fa' ch'al foco de' miei lumi
si consumi
ogni gelo, ogni durezza;
ardi poi quell'alma allora
ch'altri adora,
qual si sia, la mia bellezza.

Finis

Абзиабаратә матанеира
аҭак анасҭо
сара схаҭа арыцҳашьара сабылуазар,
Аӡәы игәаҟра сара схы-сҿи слакҭеи ччо
агәыҭра хаақәа иҭо аҭак асҭозар,
абзиабара қьиа, сгәахәтәы башахо иҟаумтцан
агәы хьшәашәа иаднамкыло,
амшын аҟәараҿоума аҧшаҳәаҿоума
агәрамгара
зынӡа исҟәатцроуп абзиабара санамоу.
Сыблақәа рымца атцаҟа
иарҧсаҳәааит
ахьшәашәареи амчра зегьи;
ари агәы иблааит нас
даҿеаӡәы, дызусҭазаалакь
абзиабара дамҿехакны дамазарц азы,
сыҧшӡара

qne^{A} nteq^{I} riq^{c}
qne^{A} tla^{f} qo^{E} nteq^{I} riq^{c}
Nga^{J} ran^{f} chaq^{f} shyaq^{c} riq^{E} renq^{E}
nga^{J} ran^{f} la^{G} chaq^{f} sqwe^{f}
sha^{f} niya^{J} ndyon^{H} qo^{E} nlo^{E} ndiya^{A} sqwe^{f} qne^{H}
lon^{L} ska^{K} ka^{G} qo^{E} shtyan^{H} ska^{J} chaq^{f},
chaq^{f} kan^{J} sqwe^{f} ti^{J}
ndon^{G} qa^{I} riq^{c} jlo^{E} qo^{E} ni^{E} qya^{J},
ja^{A} la^{E} ta^{G} chaq^{f} jyaq^{f}, ndiya^{A} chaq^{f} sqwe^{f}
no^{A} nda^{H} tykeq^{B} qin^{K} sya^{K} qnya^{K}
kyan^{J} qya^{f} ska^{A} sya^{K} tqwa^{B} qin^{K} ran^{f},
Ja^{A} la^{I} ta^{G} chaq^{f} jyaq^{f} chaq^{f} tqwa^{J} tyqa^{I} tqo^{E}
ska^{A} sya^{K} jnyi^{H} qo^{E} ndiyeq^{f} riq^{c}
ja^{A} jla^{H} sti^{J} qnya^{J} jano^{K} ndon^{G} qa^{J} renq^{H} ntyqan^{J} qin^{I}.
Nda^{G} la^{J} chaq^{f} sha^{f} kiq^{A} sqyu^{c} jlon^{H}
shti^{H} qin^{J}
ndiya^{A} na^{f} nkqwa^{G}, ndiya^{A} na^{f} tji^{J}
nda^{G} la^{J} chaq^{f} tykwen^{f} tson^{B} sya^{K}
chaq^{f} shka^{I} janq^{G} ndon^{G} qa^{J} riq^{c} tyqan^{E}
ton^{G} nga^{J} ti^{J} ka^{J}, ne^{L}.

con una sonrisa y una mirada,
no permitas, Amor gentil,
que mi ardor
sea tomado en vano por una alma helada,
no permitas que en una playa o una orilla
un corazón sin fe
me abandone enamorada.
Haz que al fuego de mis ojos
ablande
cualquier frialdad, cualquier dureza;
Deja que ese corazón arda
para que otro le adore,
quienquiera que sea, mi belleza.

si Θqohm kaar |''aan
|àe d'omase |aan nǂaqni sae
||hoa si ǂae !qhung |ai ||qahm ke
Nn ǂai |qahm
Ee ||hoa si n|ahang |ai |''aan,
||hoa n||aha koan ki N!óo ǂóéke
||hoa n||aha koan nn ǂ'ai |ai |qahm soe
N|oan ka |'aan !oni soe aan |uhum
Nn |'áan si !quhu ki |qahm kaan ǂai |ai tuu Ki aa
Xabe ke hake, Nn |qahm, Siqaye Ma'an

INTERLOCVTORI.

OVIDIO

VENERE

AMORE

APOLLO

DAFNE

NVNZIO

CHORO DI NINFE, E PASTORI.

OVIDIO.

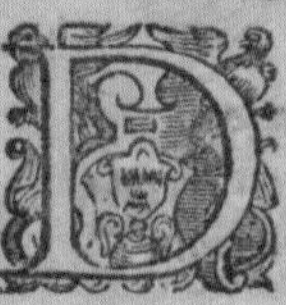

A fortunati campi, oue immortali
Godonsi all'ombra de frondosi Mirti
I graditi dal Ciel felici spirti
Mostromi in questa notte à voi mortali
Quel mi son io, che sù la dotta Lira
Cantai le fiamme de celesti amanti
Ei trasformati lor vari sembianti
Soaue sì, ch' il mondo ancor m' ammira
Indi l' arte insegnai come si deste
In vn gelato sen fiamma d' amore
E come in libertà ritorni vn' core
Cui son d'amor le fiamme aspre, e moleste.
Mà qual par che trà l' ombre, e 'l Ciel rischiari
Noua luce, e splendor di rai celesti
Qual maestà vegg' io? Son forse questi
Gl' eccelsi Augusti miei felici, e chiari?
Ah riconosco io ben l' alta Regina
Gloria, e splendor de Lotaringi Regi
Il cui nome immortal, gl' alteri fregi
Celebra 'l mondo, e 'l nobil Arno inchina.
Seguendo di giouar l' antico stile
Con chiaro esempio à dimostrarui piglio

CHORO.

Almo Dio, che'l carro ardente
Per lo ciel volgendo intorno
Vesti'l dì d'vn' aureo manto;
Se trà l'ombra orrida algente
Splend' il Ciel di lume adorno
E' pur tua la gloria, e'l vanto.
Se germoglian frondi, e fiori
Selue, e prati, e rinouella
L'ampia terra il suo bel manto,
Se de suoi dolci tesori
Ogni pianta si fà bella
E' pur tua la gloria, e'l vanto.
Per te viue, e per te gode
Quanto scerne occhio mortale
O rettor del carro eterno
Mà si taccia ogn' altra lode
Sol de l'arco, e de lo strale
Voli il grido al Ciel superno
Nobil vanto il fier Dragone
Di velen, di fiamme armato
Su'l terren versat' ha l'alma
Per trecciar fregi, e corone
Al bel crin di raggi ornato
Qual fia degno Edera, ò Palma?

Am. CHE tù vadia cercando, ò giglio, ò rosa
Per infiorarti i crini
Non ti vò creder nò madre vezzosa.
[Ven]er. Che cerco dunque ò figlio?
Am. Rosa non già ne giglio.
Cerchi d'Adone, ò d'altro viè più bello
Leggiadro Pastorello
Ven. Ah triste tristo. Ecco'l Signor di Delo
Pe' boschi hoggi sen van gli Dei del Cielo
Ap. Dimmi possente Arciero
Qual fera attendi, ò qual serpente al varco
Ch'hai la faretra, e l'arco?
Am. Se da quest' arco mio
Non fù Fitone vcciso,
Arcier non son però degno di riso,
E son del Cielo Apollo vn' nume anch'io.
Ap. Sollo, ma quando scocchi
L'arco, sbendi tù gl'occhi
O ferisci all'oscuro arciero esperto?
Ven. S'hai di saper desio
D'vn cieco arcier le proue
Chiedilo al Re dell'onde
Chiedilo in Cielo à Gioue
E trà l'ombre profonde
Del Regno orrido oscuro
Chiedi chiedi à Pluton s'ei fù sicuro?
Ap. S'in cielo, in mare, in terra
Amor trionfi in guerra
Doue, doue m'ascondo
Chi nouo Ciel mi insegna, ò nouo mondo?

Sò ben

West

!Xoon → what most people in corridors speak

'Nlohan → more in Botswana

ǂuka lâã ǂaan

1 Qxai N!aga ki Nǂahnya ki
2 Ãẽ gaye (Ee gayi)
3 Ee ǁaha !ghu si g!ahan ka ǂhaan
4 Ki si ke n!ore ke ǂai g!ahm ke? Ee kaha Sâã? (Ee sâã)
5 Oh Ee ha-ke ka huiki
6 Siǂghai ka tshari taam ki tshai gai (') Nn n)
7 Aa ke hake ke si 'obe ki sai ke (ǁahan)
8 Aa ke ǁahan? Aa ki G!ohu Delos lai (Nn n)
9 Aa ǂaha ka tahba? (Appolo) Nn ǂaha
10 Aa ǂaha ka tahba Nǂoha gaye
11 Sin!ohan ka kaan aan !uri. (N!ahi)

Nǂuri se laa ǂaan

1 Aa ki G!uhu ki si
2 N!ari Kii
3 Ee si gain N!ore
4 Som hanti ka ǁahang
5 N!ori ǂae ǁang ǂae N!ahin sae
6 Aa !ai N!ari saen si si G⊙ohm kaan
7 Nǂahni ii ka si gara. N⊙aha saa na ki tun gayan
10 N⊙ahan ka si gain ka tan ke
11 Aa G!uhu ki G!ahin ki
12 Tahng N!ahoeke kaan si n!aan !aan 'ke si G'xaru
13 Ki G!uhu 'uni
14 O G!uhu ki Nǂahan ka !ai
15 Xaka !Ju aa !uru ka !ahin nn ǂahang
16 Siisi G!ohong tahbe laa gxaan
17 Oh Nǁahri ii !ahon G⊙aghm
18 Ji Nǂuhmi ki taam ki ǂaan !aan
19 Ji si tshuum ǂagi !aa tshuum saa ke N!ore saan

20 Ee si gain-gain 21 ki !hau-!hausi
22 Oahi haka ki gaha ki taam? G!ǁaha ǂae ǁaa

ǁahise laa ǂaan

(Clicks)
(⊙) 1 Ee ǁahan ǁhoa si⊙gxohm ke
(|) 2 !uhung ke ee 'oe ke si⊙gxobe
(!) 3 Xata ee !hoa Nǂung N!ae ki khanjae: Ee !ahan N!aga
(ǁ) 4 G!uhu kaõ si N!uni ka kahang ki tau ki kahan kaan
(ǂ) 5 Aa n!ahi ǁaa ki !agm ke aa kaa ǁaa Kii
6 Khobe aa !ahan ki N!ahi xaba
7 !aham ee ka Khaoxa, !aham ii ka ǂahni !ai ke Ii ki ǂaha

haka se !aa ǂaan

(1) Thai Nǁaghang ka gain ka
(2) Kng na ke n!aan !aan 'oni! (3) G!ǁaha ee tshare tam nn saan !ohong ka G!agri kaan
(4) Ee Nǂuhung ka n!ahi si ǁagba (5) Aa koekã garu
(6) Nn se Nǂubisike !ai Nǂahni
(7) Ee gai !ae si N!uhi ke kuru ka nǁahba gae ke
(8) Ee ǁahntu (Diana) (9) !Ju !oe silose n!ae ee !au Nǁohung
(10) Nn ǁhoa ki !ahbi, ha-aan nn ki g!ugung
(11) Xata ee !aa tshuumsa ka gain ka a dei N⊙hai

Korose laa ǂaan

(1) Silagan ke gain ke ee si !agba
(2) Ee si gara nn ǁhoa !ai ǁai ki ǂo'oki
(3) Ke !ae taa ka sa ke ǂaha ghuu ǂae si Nǁause
(4) Aa !uan G⊙xohm

①

① first

①. Drink the Black Blood
②. To kill it, Killed him
③ You are making fun out of me,
④ at our Country that have Peace, and love?
Where is he going? (he's gone)
⑤ Who will help us
⑥. the snake will bite us (we)
(7) Who are you to tell us (snake)
(8) You snake? You are Delos God (we)
9 he shoot the arrow? (Appolo) (he Shoot)
10. he shoot the arrow are Killed
11. It is the the Killer (snake)

② Second ②

1 You are our God
2 from heaven
3 he Decorated the world and heavens
4 the shadow is very cold
5. the world has light and it shines
6 your world makes me happy
7 And th. the trees get flowers and leaves
(8,9) And the trees are so beautiful
10 And trees has Decorated themselves and looks beautiful
11 You are Indeed great God
12 Everything that we see and touch goes through you.
13. through God
14 Oh you most high God
15. You never left us
16. We are looking for a Bow and Arrow
17. Oh is happy
18 Lets prepared us
19. We Breath out your soul, in the world
20. he Decorated
21 his Eye brows

③ third ③

1. he is very happy
(2) Now he is Enjoying his happy life
(3) But he still Not believing
(4) God want us to do so on Earth
(5) Your love is always there
(6) tomorrow and heart calm down
(7) Love, Chief), Love is Everything

④ fourth ④

① Everything that is beautiful
② Which I have seen with my Eyes
3 the tree that it hairs has turned into White leaves
④ the foot prints that running Now
⑤ has disappers
⑥ And they gets roots and branches
⑦ Maybe she yust wanted to remain a Virgin
⑧ her Godess (Diana)
⑨ give her strenght, Power to remain like that
⑩ I'am Not, No I'am sad
⑪ but her wonderful soul turns into a tree

Venus

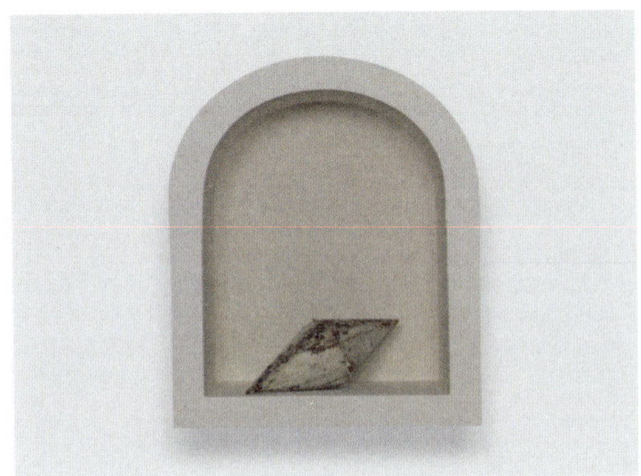

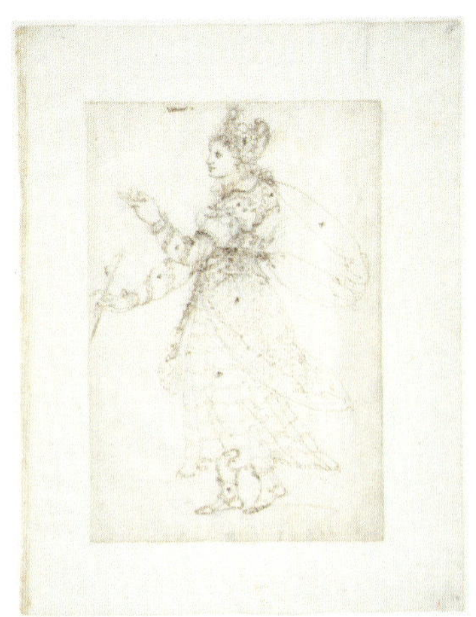

Cupid

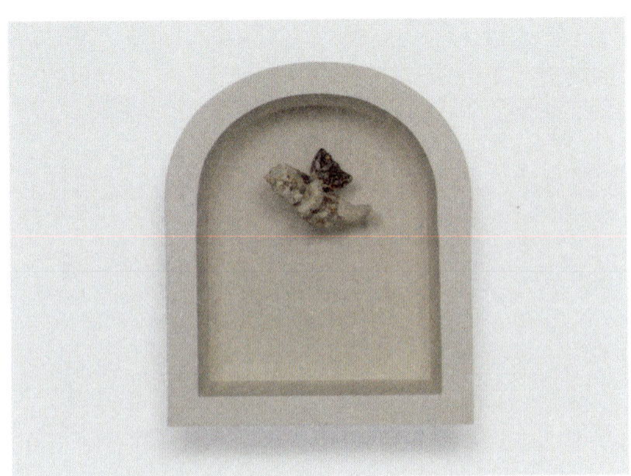

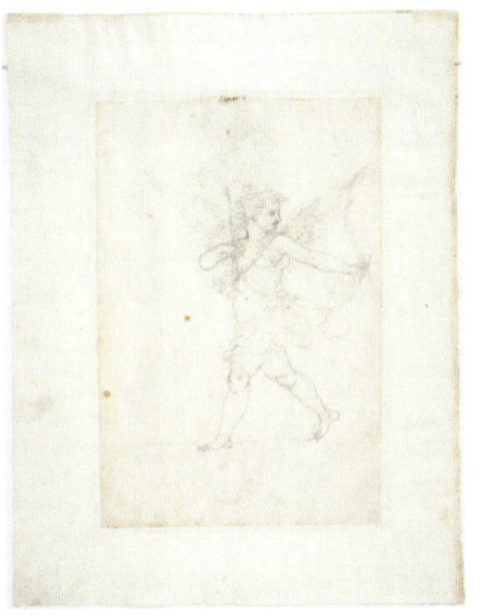

dafne phono libretto 2

Wherein the translations from Libretto 1
are re-translated word for word into English.

[Prologue]

Ovid
From the joyful fields, where the immortals
enjoy, in the shade of the leafy myrtle trees,
the blessed, happy spirits of Heaven,
I appear before you mortals tonight.
I am he who to the learned lyre
sang of the passions of divine lovers,
and of their figures metamorphosized,
so sweetly that the world still admires me.
Then I taught the art of how
the flame of Love is kindled in an icy breast,
and of how liberty is restored to a heart
plagued by the harsh and vexing flames of Love.
Now continuing to follow the ancient style,
by clear example do I seek to show you,
Lords and Ladies, how dangerous it is
to treat as nothing the power of Love.
You will witness the tears of that god who in heaven
bears in his fine golden carriage light to the day,
and see him worship the bright spirit of his beloved
nymph
within the transformed tree-trunk.

[First chorus]

Chorus. *(Echo.)*
Drunk with blood in this dark wood
just now lay the terrible beast. *(He was!)*
So he no longer poisons
our lovely countryside? Has he gone elsewhere?
(Gone!)
Alas, who will defend us
if the wicked beast should return today? *(I!)*
Who are you who reassure and console us?

[First chorus]

Chorus. *(Echo.)*
In this dark wood laid
Drunk with blood to death, ugly beast.
Would it poison more
our lovely village? Has he moved and gone else-
where?
But, who will protect us then
if the evil beast should return today?
Who are you to soothe and comfort us? (*The sun!)*

People singing. *(Leaving voice.)*
Drunk and covered blood laying down inside wood
here,
This how laying beast that one now. *(Laying down
then)*
Now no more give poison
Inside countryside that beautiful ours left another
village? *(Left)*
Alas, who is do care us now

[Prologue]

Ovid
The fabled band of the gods, whom the myrtle
shades with its leaves,
Swelled by the spirits of the blessed dead, comes
together in blissful company.
Lately from those fields of Elysium whose harvest
is joy
Have I come to address your ears, who are bound
to die.
It was I whose budding poems the learned lyre
assisted to recount
What are the loves of those above, what are the
shapes those sacred powers shift.
Such was the merit of my song, so great was its
piercing sweetness
That fame in the poet's craft has not yet failed me.
I am he who once taught the artful flame to conquer
Hearts held fast by ice; no less that savage fury to
be appeased
By which Cupid holds thrall the hearts he binds.
Nor will the weapons of the antique Muse cease
their work
While you still have perils to run
O my lords and ladies, beneath the yoke of the
tyrant Love:
Which it is my burden to show you by an example
of note
Lest in your minds you should treat their power
lightly.
Wonders will be shown you: how the eyes grow
dark with tears
Of one who has the power to renew the course of
the Sun in his chariot
And how that bringer of gold, outstanding in

Chorus. *(Echo)*
Drunk with blood in this obscure forest
now lies the terrible beast *(There it was!)*
So that it does not poison
our beautiful countryside? Has he gone to another
place? *(Gone!)*
Woe to us! Who will defend us
if the evil beast came back today? *(I!)*
Who are you that gives us trust and comfort?

[First]

Drink the black blood
To kill it, killed him
You are making fun out of me
At our country that have peace and love?
Where is he going? *(He's gone)*
Who will help us
The snake will bite us *(we)*
Who are you to tell us *(snake)*
You snake? You are Delos God *(we)*

(The Sun!)
Are you the Sun? Are you the god of Delos? *(I!)*
Have you your bow with you to strike him, Apollo? *(I have it!)*
If you have your bow, shoot to death
this cruel monster who devours us. *(Now!)*

Are you the Sun? Are you the god of Delosians? *(I!)*
Do you have the bow to strike him, Apollo? *(I have it!)*
If you have the bow, kill
this cruel monster who devours us. *(Now!)*

if returns beast that one now then? *(I!)*
Who are you because console us?
Is you is god Sun? Is god Delos is? *(I!)*
Apollo, have bow with you so hurt to? *(I have it!)*
If have bow with you, kill more to
monster this much more suffering doing to us. *(Now!)*

The Python and Apollo on stage.
The Python is dead.

[First scene]

Apollo
The evil dragon at last lies dead
on the bloodstained earth,
slain by my invincible bow.
Go in safety to the meadow,
nymphs and shepherds, go safely to the woods.
No more with flames and poison
will his horrible breath infect the pure heavens.
Let the beautiful roses return to
your loving cheeks;
let your heart be easy, your face calm.
I have taken the soul and breath from the cruel serpent.

[Second chorus]

Chorus
Divine God, who in your fiery chariot
goes riding through the sky,
bedeck the day with a golden mantle.
If amid horrible, freezing shadows
the sky is radiant with light,
yours indeed is the glory and pride.
If leaves and flowers blossom,

[Second chorus]

Chorus
The almighty God,
who in his fiery chariot goes riding through the sky,
bedeck our day with a golden mantle.
If amid horrible, freezing shadows
the sky is radiant with light,
yours indeed is the glory and pride.
If leaves and flowers blossom,

People singing
The main, who is inside metal shining
flying passing going sky,
bedeck day with one cloth shining
When happen horrible, happen light freezing
hanging light look sky,
you indeed who glory pride.
like leaves with flowers have blossom it

worship, as suitor of a half-goddess
Pays court to her spirit, newly encased in earth-
bound bark.

(The sun!)
Are you the sun? Are you the god of Delos? *(I!)*
Do you bring the bow with you to hurt him, Apolo?
(I have it!)
If you have your bow, shoot to death
to this cruel monster that devours us. *(Now!)*

He shoot the arrow? (Apollo) he shoots
He shoot the arrow are killed
It is the killer *(snake)*

[Second]

Chorus
God divine, who in your carriage of fire
promenades around all of heaven,
dress the day of a golden mantle.
If between the horrible frozen shadow
the sky shines with your light,
yours also are the glory and the pride.
If blossom leaves and flowers,

You are our God
From heaven
He decorated the world and heavens
The shadow is very cold
The world has light and it shines
Your world makes me happy
And the trees get flowers and leaves

and woods and fields, and
the vast earth renews its fair mantle;
if with its sweet treasures
every plant adorns itself
yours indeed is the glory and pride.
Through you lives and enjoys
the mortal eye all that it discerns,
o ruler of the eternal chariot.
But all other praise should be left aside;
only of the bow and the arrow
should the cry rise to the highest heavens.
Noble praise! The proud dragon,
armed with venom and with flames,
has poured out its soul upon the earth.
To weave garlands and crowns
for the beautiful brow arrayed with rays,
which is the worthier: the laurel or the palm?

[Second scene]

Cupid and Venus

Cupid
That you go seeking lilies or roses
to deck your hair,
I cannot believe you, no, fair mother.

Venus
What then do I seek, my son?

Cupid
Neither rose nor lily:
you seek Adonis or some other more handsome
delightful shepherd.

and woods and fields, and
the vast earth renews its fair mantle;
if it adorns with treasure treasures
every plant
yours indeed is the glory, our shiny pride.
O, you, ruler of the immortal chariot
Through you lives and enjoys the death's
eye.
But all other praise should be left aside;
only of the bow and the arrow should be lifted
the cry of which rises to heavens.
Noble praise!
armed with venom and with flames, the proud
dragon's
soul poured and fell upon the earth.
Crowns should be weaved
for the beautiful brow arrayed with rays,
which would fit more: made of the laurel or palm
leaves?

[Second scene]

Cupid and Venus

Cupid
Lilies or roses do you seek
to beautify your hair,
Fair mother, I cannot trust you

Venus
What then do I seek, my son?

Cupid
Neither rose nor lily:
you seek Adonis or some other more handsome
delightful shepherd.

and inside woods with inside field, and
and earth renews thing its mantle; each one it and
treasure sweet that
and each one plant do adorns to
you are who glory pride.
Through happy you came light earth
everything discerns to seed rock face mortal
sacred who orders everything eternal
Everything who is not praise must have left aside
only bow and arrow that use them and bow only
that
must cry prayers ours rise further heaven.
Praise noble sitting. Animal big that takes out fire,
armed with venom and flames,
poured soul on earth
For weave garlands with thing on head
for on mouth head that hang rays
who is worthier: laurel or palm?

Cupid and star evening

Cupid
go seek more flower rose or orchids
to deck hair yours
no believe me you, no, fair mother,

Cupid
Nor flower rose nor flower lilies
going seek to Adonis or that other man handsome is
like one shepherd who good speak

Cupid
Even animal dragon

Forests and fields, and
the entire earth renews its beautiful mantle; if with its
sweet treasures,
all the plants embellish
yours also are the glory and the pride.
Through you lives and rejoices
All that perceives the mortal eye,
oh governor of the eternal chariot.
Nevertheless all the praise should be put aside;
only the bow and the arrow
if the shout rises to the heavens more high.
Noble glory! The dragon honored
armed with venom and flames,
has poured its soul on the earth.
To braid garlands and crowns
on the beautiful forehead adorned with rays,
Which will be more worthy, the laurel or the palm?

And the trees are so beautiful
And trees he's decorated themselves and looks beautiful
You are indeed great God
Everything that we see one touch goes through you.
Through God
Oh you most high God
You never left us
We are looking for a Bow and Arrow
Oh is happy
Lets prepared us
We breathe out your soul, in the world
He decorated
His eye brows

Cupid and Venus

Cupid
That you go looking for lilies or roses
to adorn your hair
I don't want to believe, no, beautiful
mother.

Venus
Then what am I looking for, son?

Cupid
Neither rose, nor lily:
search for Adonis, or another still

Cupid and Venus

Cupid
What are you searching for roses
flowers to decorate yourself. I don't
believe you my cute mum

Venus
What do you think I am searching for
my child

Cupid
You are not looking for roses flowers,
you are looking for Adonis or a

Venus
Oh, woe, woe! Here is the lord of Delos:
today all the gods of heaven are passing through the woods.

Apollo, Cupid and Venus

Apollo
Tell me, mighty archer,
what wild beast do you await, or what serpent to ambush,
such that you bear the quiver and bow?

Cupid
Even if the dragon
was not slain by my bow,
I am not an archer still deserving scorn,
but I too, Apollo, am a god of the heavens.

Apollo
That I know; but when you draw
the bow, do you uncover your eyes,
or do you shoot blindly, expert archer?

Cupid
Yes, you will know it for sure!

Apollo
Oh, you are wrong to get angry:
either forgive me, Love,
or, if you wish to wound me, spare my heart.

Cupid
I know well that you do not fear
the power of a child,
o slayer of monsters and serpents,

Venus
Oh, woe, woe! Here is the lord of Delos:
today all the gods of heaven are passing through the woods.

Cupid
Even if the dragon was not slain by my bow,
I am not a scorn-deserving archer,
I am, Apollo, a god of the heavens.

Cupid
Yes, you will for sure, understand it!

Cupid
I know you do not fear the power of a child,
o, slayer of ugly monsters and serpents,
but you are still making fun and sport of me.

Venus
You will see what danger is under it to joke with him,
even though he is little, naked and blind.

no died with bow mine,
good do archer not give laugh you to me,
but I, Apollo, I am god of heaven

Cupid
Yes, know for sure

Cupid
Know well me that no fear you
power of child
is one person slayer who kills monsters and snakes,
no stop that making fun and sport at me

more beautiful and
charming shepherd.

Venus
Oh, well, well! Here is the lord of
Delos:
today all the gods of the heaven pass
through the forests.

Apollo, Cupid, and Venus

Cupid
Even if the dragon
did not die by my bow
I am not an archer that still deserves
contempt
but still I, Apollo, am a god of the
heavens.

Cupid
Yes, you will know with certainty!

Cupid
I know well that you do not have fear
of the strength of a child
oh, murderer of monsters and
serpents,
still, you make fun of me and it
entertains you.

handsome shepherd or handsome
gentleman

Venus
Oh no no, it is Delos the God
Today God and the world will walk
through the trees

Apollo, Cupid, and Venus

Cupid
I don't care whether I will not
kill the dragon with my arrow,
but I am Cupid, I am also God

Cupid
Yes you will know who I am,
although I am small, you are just
making fun from me.

Cupid
I know that and I believed that you
are a hero and powerful and you are
making fun just because I am a child
and you killer of big
snakes and dragon

Venus
You will see what will happen
to you although he is a
child you will see with your tube eyes

but you are still making fun and sport of me.

Venus
You will see what a grave risk it is to joke with him,
even though he is a little boy, naked and blind.

[Third chorus]

Chorus
He who lives unfettered by the bonds of love,
let him enjoy his liberty happily,
but not arrogantly: wrapped in a dark cloud
for us is the high decree of heaven.
If now you feel neither little nor much of Love,
tomorrow you will have a disturbed and restless heart,
and you will find to be a cruel and harsh master
that Love, whom you so haughtily disdained before.

[Third chorus]

Chorus
He who lives unfettered by love,
let him enjoy his liberty happily,
but not arrogantly: wrapped in a dark cloud
with the high decree shown from heavens.
If you don't have even a little Love,
tomorrow you will have a restless heart,
and you will find to be harsh
and cruel master
that you've always disdained.

people singing
He unfettered who bonds of love world
allow you that walks happy alone
but not do arrogant: wrapped in cloud dark
for us came heaven open to us
now sad more feels you
tomorrow disturbed and restless heart yours is
you will wonder because is one master cruel and harsh
that love, whom give haughtily disdained you before.

[Third scene]

Dafne, Apollo and Cupid

Dafne
Of the fugitive deer
this is the very footprint impressed:
if only the beast itself was here nearby.

Apollo
What gentle light of lovely eyes
reaches my heart?
Lovely nymph, what are you looking around for?

[Third scene]

Dafne, Apollo and Cupid

Dafne
This footprint
Belongs to the fugitive deer
if only the beast itself was here nearby.

Dafne
If some beast in this dark forest
Is wandering, thus I look

Dafne, Apollo and Cupid

Dafne
of to deer who fugitive
is that here is impressed footprint:
if wondering beast that nearby here.

Dafne
looking I if some beast
wondering inside forest dark this.

[Third]

Chorus
He who lives unchained from the bonds of love,
May he enjoy happily his freedom,
but not proud: wrapped in a obscure cloud
for us it is the high decree of heaven.
If now you feel neither little nor much love,
tomorrow you will have a heart disturbed and restless,
and you will find that the owner cruel and severe
it is Love, which before you unappreciated so proudly.

He is very happy
Now he is enjoying his happy life
But he still not believing
God want us to do so on Earth
Your love is always there
Tomorrow and heart calm down
Love, chief, love is everything

Dafne, Apollo, and Cupid

Dafne
Of the fugitive deer,
this is the same footprint imprinted:
if only the beast same was nearby.

Dafne
I am looking if any beast
is wandering in this obscure forest.

Dafne, Apollo, and Cupid

Dafne
The footprint of the springbok
that are here, I guest it were here now

Dafne
I am looking for animals but
I don't have an idea where
Has gone to

Dafne
I am looking if some beast
was wandering in this dark forest.

Apollo
Without hurling your arrows or drawing your bow,
scouring valleys or mountains,
can you take a noble prey with your lovely eyes.

Dafne
I covet no other prey, no other delight
than wild beasts and woods; and I am content and happy
if I shoot a wandering doe or savage boar.

Apollo
I, too, can draw the bow,
and if it does not displease you,
let us agree to have a delightful hunt together.

Dafne
Other than my arrow,
I do not want any companion; farewell.

Apollo
Alas, be not so hasty:
wait, nymph, wait.

Cupid
See, how I have managed to trap you.
Oh, learn what it is to disdain my age and bow!

Dafne
Except wild beasts of woods and the woods
I know no other delight; then if there's a wandering doe
and a savage boar I can kill, another delight
I don't have.

Dafne
Other than my arrow,
I do not want any companion; farewell.

Cupid
See, how I have managed to trap you.
Oh, learn what it is to disdain my age and bow!

Dafne
no want me other prey, nor another thing delight
beast wild and inside woods; content and happy me
If shoot to doe who goes running or I shoot a wild boar

Dafne
with bow this mine,
no need another companion come with me, I am leaving.

Cupid
already saw now? felt you inside trap.
Oh, already saw thing happens because give joke you elder and bow

Dafne
I covet no other prey, another delight
more than the beasts and the forests;
and I am content and happy
shooting a wandering doe or a wild
boar.

Dafne
Besides my arrow,
I do not want company; until forever.

Dafne
But I am not looking for another
Animal, but I will be very excited
If I kill bush pig or another
Animal

Dafne
Me and my bow and arrow
We will be fine we
Don't want to be with someone

Cupid
From now on you have to
know that although me and my
bow and arrow are small but
still we are heroes.

[Fourth chorus]

Chorus
What new marvel
have my eyes seen! Into tree-like fronds
blonde hair turned,
and the foot that just now ran fast and loose,
buried in the ground,
sprouting branches and leaves.
Perhaps in response to chaste desires
the sacred goddess [Diana]—since fleeing was in
vain—
offered such aid,
not as punishment, no, but for mercy
did she change so beautiful a soul into a new bush.

[Fourth scene]

Apollo
So this rough bark
will always enclose her heavenly beauty?
Eyes, you who saw
the sublime beauty which forces you to weep,
gaze too at these branches;
here lies and here is hidden
my love, my heart, my treasure,
for whom, although immortal, I languish and die.
Scornful and shy nymph,
who, fleeing from the love of a heavenly god,
changed your beautiful form into a green laurel,
let it never be that I shall not honour and love you,
for always on my golden brow
will your leaves and branches make a garland.
But oh, if within these branches
you hear my weeping, listen to my noble lyre,
and what gifts it beseeches for you from heaven.

[Fourth chorus]

Chorus
What new marvel
have my eyes seen!
Into tree-like fronds blonde hair turned,
and the foot that just now ran fast,
buried in the ground,
sprouting branches and leaves..
Perhaps the sacred goddess (Diana)
in response to chaste desires—since fleeing was in
vain
as it was understood—offered such aid,
not as punishment, no, but for mercy
did she change so beautiful a soul into a plant.

people singing
dear beautiful more looks this
saw seed rock face this, into leaves tree green
hanging hair blonde head.
and loose fast foot ran by
buried inside soil
sprouting thing branches and leaves
Perhaps in response because chaste desires
who is goddess [Diana]—in vain took off
offered aid to
no punishment, no, is because mercy
changed beautiful soul and another bush green?

[Fourth]

Chorus
What a new wonder
my eyes have seen! In fronds that look like trees
the hair blonde has turned,
and the foot that just ran fast and free,
buried in the ground,
sprouting branches and leaves...
Perhaps in response to the limpid desires
the sacred goddess [Diana]—since fleeing was in vain—
she offered such help,
not as a punishment, no, but for mercy
she changed a beautiful soul into a bush.

Everything that is beautiful
Which I have seen with my eyes
The tree that it hairs has turned into white leaves
The footprints that running now
Has disappeared
And they gets roots and branches
Maybe she just wanted to remain a virgin
Her goddess (Diana)
Give her strength, power to remain like that
I am not, no I am sad
But her wonderful soul turns into a tree

Let my tree not fear either fire or frost,
and let its eternal finery be of bright emerald,
nor shall the wrath of heaven ever hurt it again.
Let the fine swans of Dirce and the sovereign rulers
bear on their famous brows
as a sign of honour garlands and wreaths from its
green boughs.
Never shall the shepherd nor his flock, tiring
of your green mantle, strip and rob you of it:
in its welcome shadow, let nymphs and goddesses,
singing happily, pass the happy, joyous day.

[Fifth chorus]

Chorus
Beautiful, fleeing nymph,
freed and divested
of your noble, mortal form,
rejoice, young tree,
chaste and beautiful,
dear to the world and dear to heaven.
You do not worry about storm-clouds or thunder;
you crown
swans, kings and heavenly gods;
whether the sky freezes, or flames and warms,
with emeralds
ever do you happily dress and adorn yourself.
So enjoy such distinguished garments;
your virtues
do I not envy nor desire.
For if ever I am struck by Love's
golden arrow,
I will not go to war with a god.
If I stir my feet to flee
a true lover,
proud and cruel against Love,

[Fifth chorus]

Chorus
Beautiful, fleeing nymph,
divested of your noble, mortal form,
rejoice,
chaste and beautiful young tree,
matching to the world and to heaven.
About storm-clouds or thunder;
You don't fear
you crown them (give their kinghood)
swans, kings and heavenly gods;
whether the sky freezes, or flames enough to warm
you,
whatever happens you happily adorn yourself with
beautiful dress
and emeralds (with green stones).
Enjoy your
distinguished virtues (respect/worth)
I do not desire with envy.
For if ever I am struck by Love's arrow,
I will not make war against a god.
If disliking love, and merciless,
to a true lover of mine,

people singing
beautiful, nymph going hiding,
freed and divested them to
good heart yours, because you are mortal
tree new, tree baby standing only,
chaste you, beautiful
dear it world and heaven.
no worry you about hanging clouds dark and
thunder
forehead sitting you head
bird swan, king, and sacred father;
whether freezes, or will get warm heaven with
flames,
with rock green precious
every day happy good cloth and do adorns yourself
give more pleasure you with everything;
and strength have you
no want and no envy me with that
Arrive one day want love
bow golden
no going fight with sacred our god.
if stir feet because will run flee

[Fifth]

Chorus
Beautiful nymph fugitive,
freed and stripped
of your noble form mortal,
Rejoice, young tree,
chaste and beautiful,
loved by the world and loved by the heaven.
You don't worry about the clouds of storm or thunder;
you crown
swans, kings and gods celestial;
if the sky freezes, or catches in flames and heats,
with emeralds
adorn yourself and dress happy always.
Enjoy your distinctions;
your virtues
that I neither envy nor desire.
Because if I am ever surprised by Love
with his golden arrow,

The beautiful young woman is running
She is happy and not in sorrow
Because she is a woman being
She is happy
Her beauty makes me happy
The world and the Earth loves you
You don't worry about the thunder and the clouds
She crowns her just to show love
Dove, chiefs and the heavenly God
She doesn't care about world and its hardness
With the black diamonds
Everyday you are getting happy because you are leaving your life
Water with beauty
With your beautify manner
I am not jealous for what you are doing
Even if you strike me
With the shooting arrow
I am not fighting with God
I will not run
You never understand how sad I am

may my golden hair become
not like a laurel
but, rather, scrawny grass.
May my blonde hair become lowly stalks
that the voracious
flock always breaks off and scatters around,
let it be lowly hay to which the brutal teeth
of herds are drawn by greedy hunger
But if in answer to sighing,
amorous pleas,
I sparkle and burn with pity,
if I promise to another's suffering
sweet hope
with a smile and a glance,
do not permit, gracious Love,
that my ardour
is taken in vain by a cold heart,
do not allow that on a beach or a shore
a faithless heart
should abandon me when I am in love.
Let it be that at the fire of my eyes
is softened
all coldness, all harshness;
let that heart then burn
so that another should adore,
whomever he might be, my beauty.

End

if I stir my feet to flee
may my golden hair
become not like a laurel
but, rather, scrawny grass.
May my blonde hair become lowly stalks
that the voracious
flock always breaks off and scatters around,
let it be lowly hay to which the brutal teeth
of herds
are drawn by greedy hunger.
But if in answer to sighing,
amorous pleas,
I sparkle and burn with pity,
if I promise to another's suffering
sweet hope with a smile and a glance,
do not permit, gracious Love,
that my ardour is taken in vain by a cold heart,
do not allow that on a beach or a shore
a faithless heart
should abandon me when I am in love.
Let it be that at the fire of my eyes
is softened
all coldness, all harshness;
let that heart then burn
so that another should adore,
whomever he might be,
my beauty.

one people who want true to me
strong and big do me for things love I
golden become hear my head
no is it flower laurel
but, good more if become it grass scrawny
maybe hair golden my head become it stalk tree
 shadow
that animal voracious
all animals breaks familiar and scatters around,
let it be be hay to rock teeth
animal hungry
animal mean and hungry
It is thing sighing them
it is pleas good
sparkle is I stand and notice all good do
took out one promise and put one thing,
so come good only
happy face and glance
no permit, everything love
who give ardour to heart mine
will come have one heart cold to
not allow that mouth ocean
one heart lair and jesting
no abandon me when happy more me see to
allow that light fire see face
softened is
all coldness, all harshness
give more that burn heart
so another then adore
whoever is, my beauty.

I will not fight with a god.
If I move my feet to escape
of a true lover,
proud and cruel against the Love,
that my hair golden does not turn
like a laurel
but, rather, grass disembodied.
But if in response to a sigh,
and loving pleas,
I shine and burn with mercy,
if I promise the suffering of others
sweet hope
with a smile and a look,
do not permit, gentle Love,
that my burning
be taken in vain by a frozen soul,
don't permit that beach or a shore
a heart without faith
abandon me in love.
Make the fire of my eyes
soften
any coldness, any hardness;
Let the heart burn
for another to adore him,
whoever you are, my beauty.

With my decorated hair
That's my hair
But it looks like grass that has been scattered
With a short hairs
Were you hungry like that
Like animals that have stayed long without eating
He's not hungry
It's dead
With food
She's more excited
With my love please
I felt in love with you
I believed in you
I am excited
With a smile
With a breaking heart, and love
I have love
She doesn't care about me
And you should take me to the beach
Don't leave me, I am in love with you
With the fire that is in my eyes
My heart burns with love, because the love I have
with people, but who I love (my beauty)

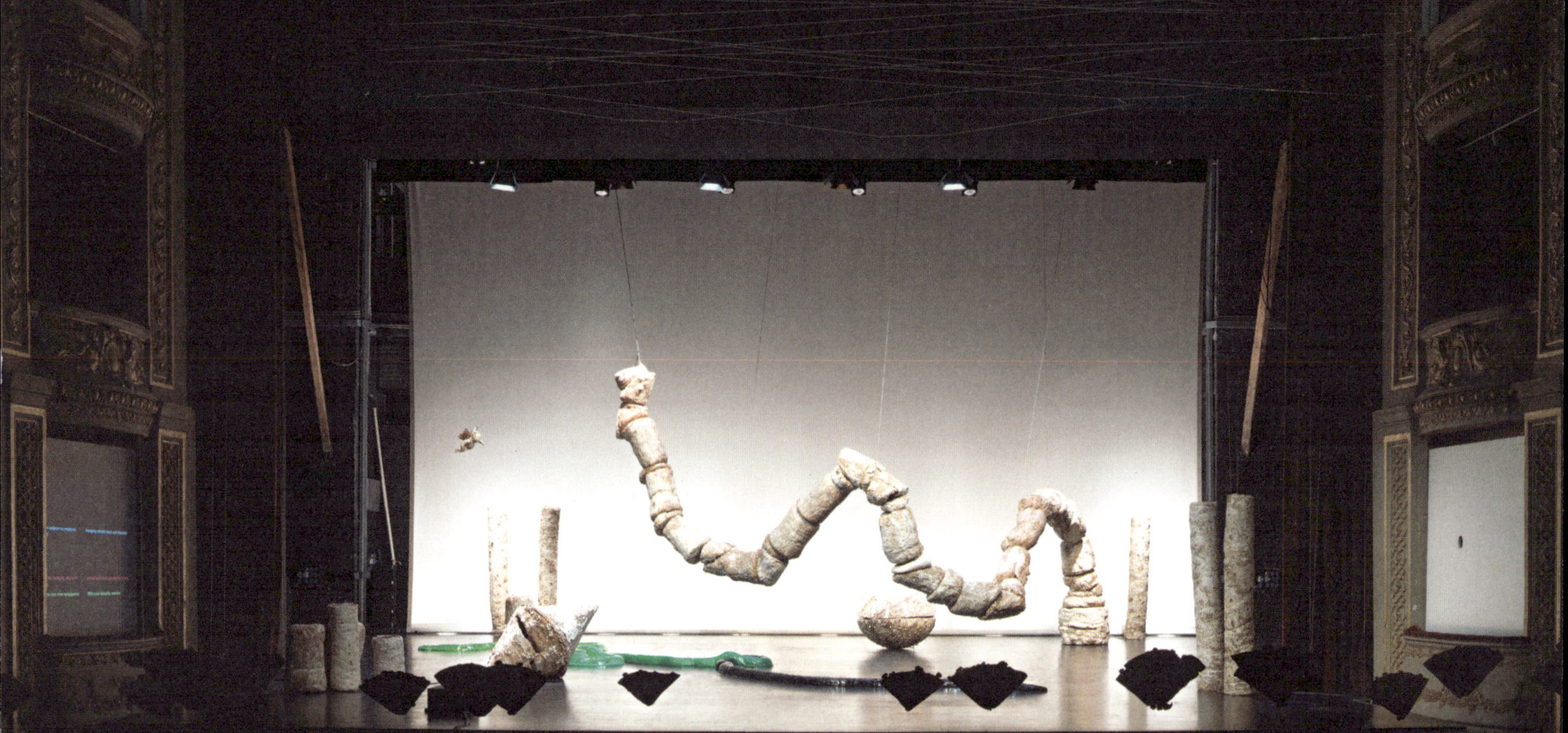

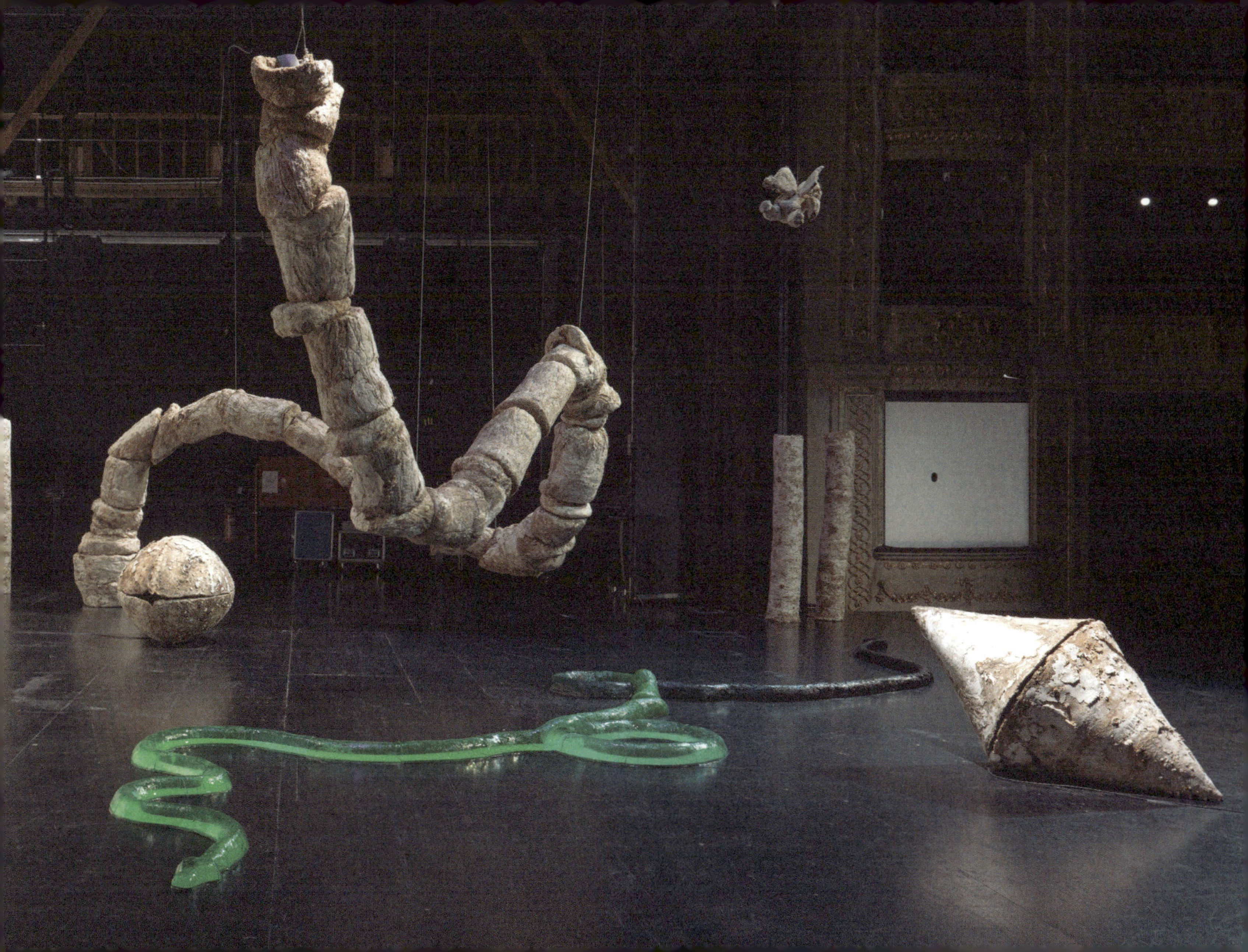

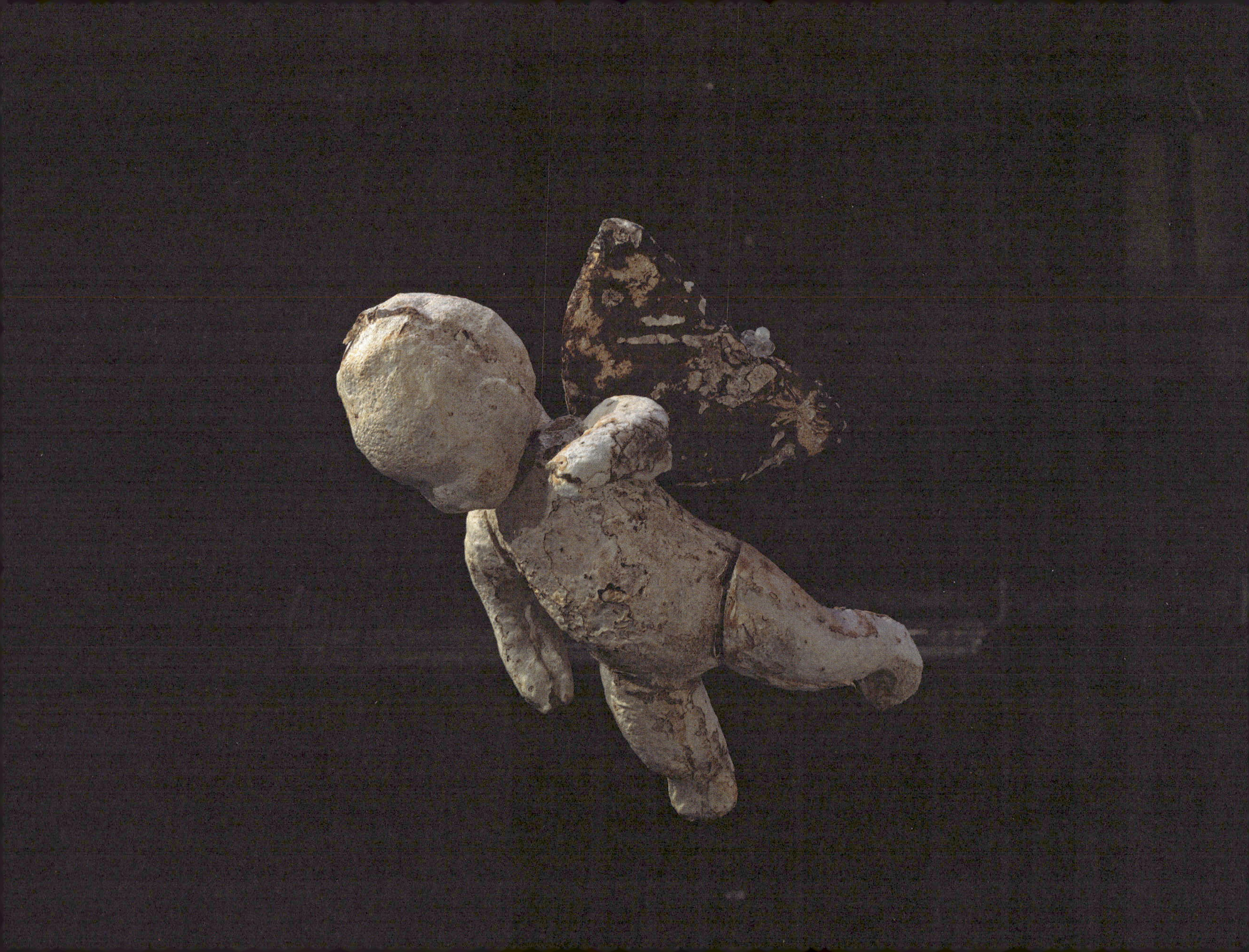

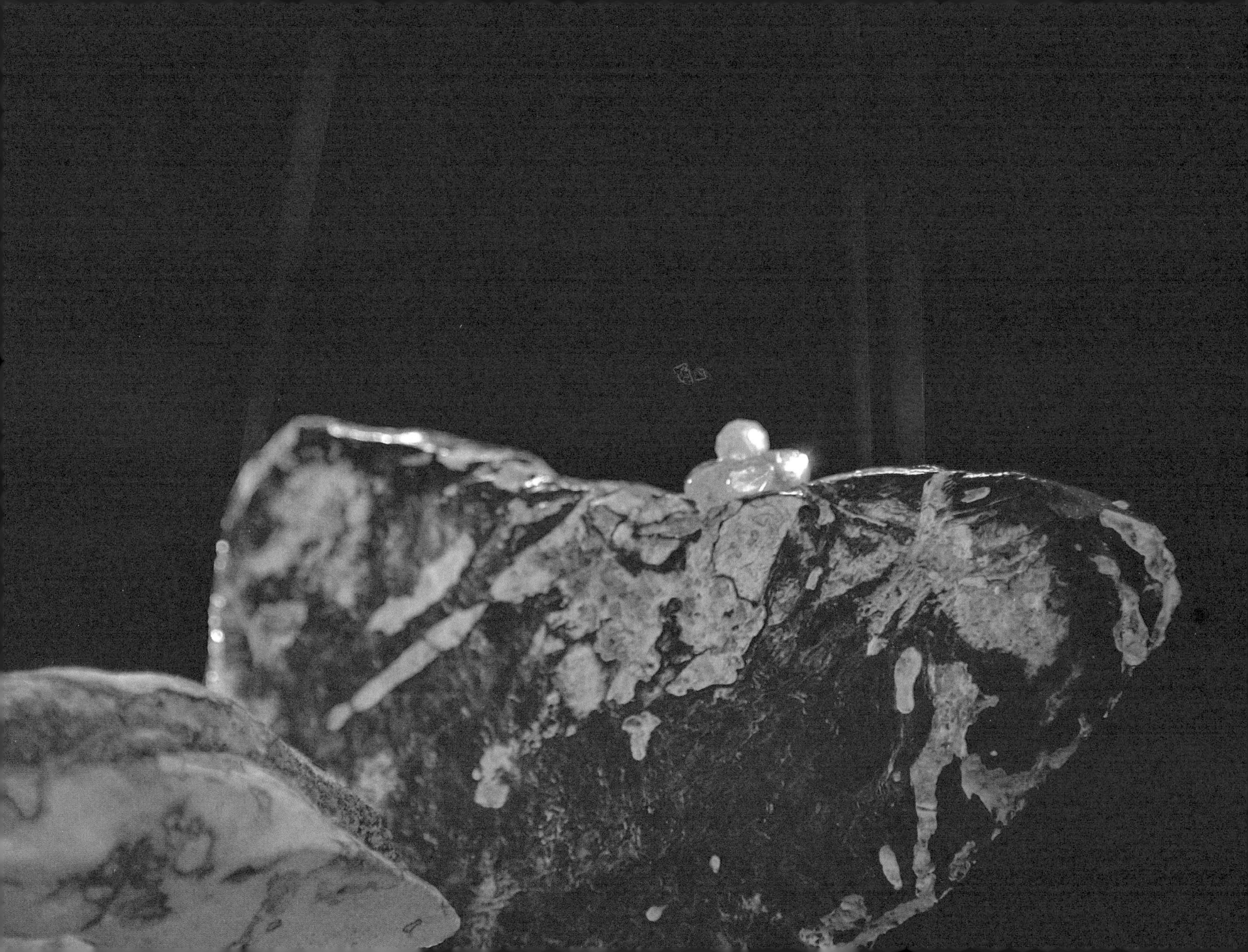

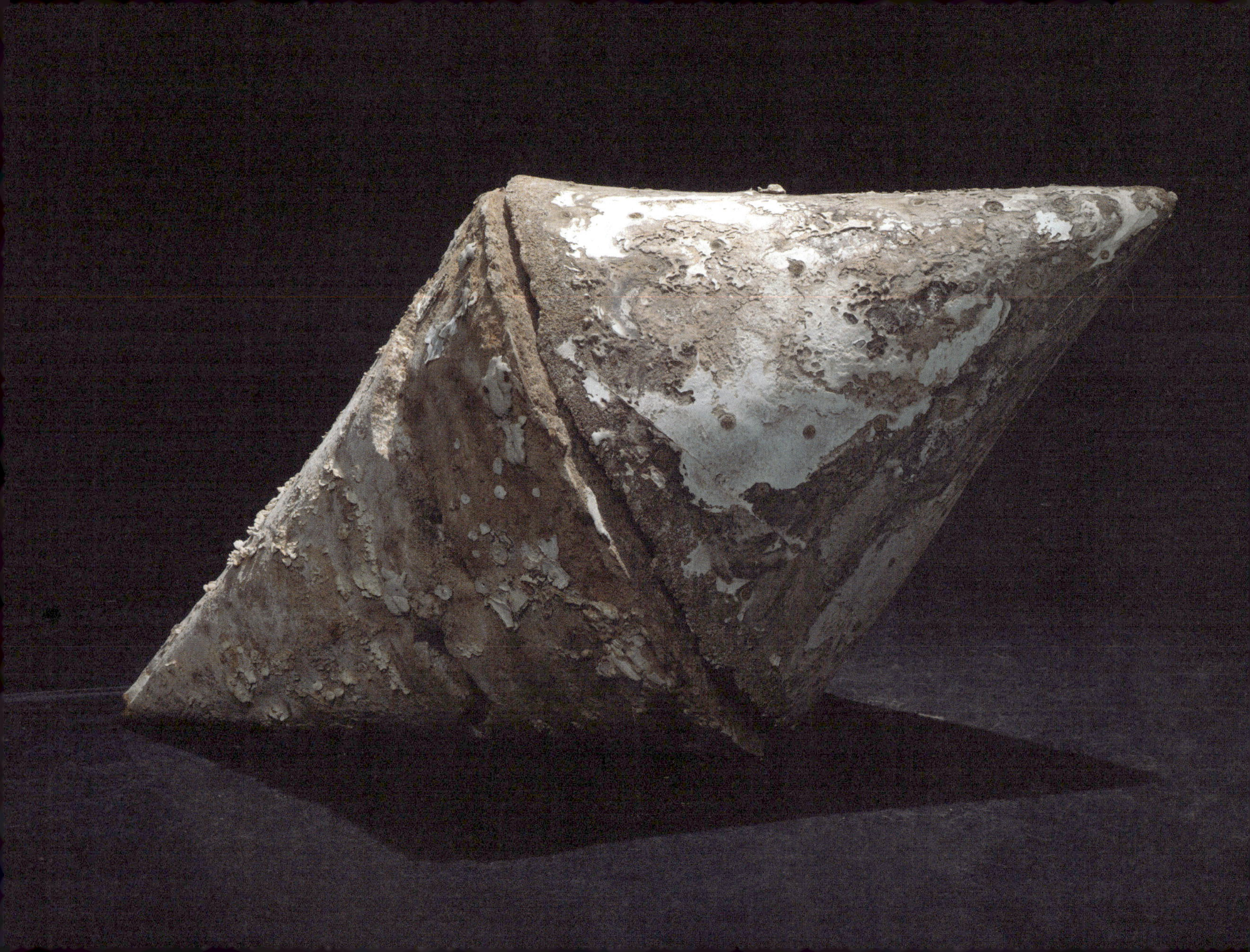

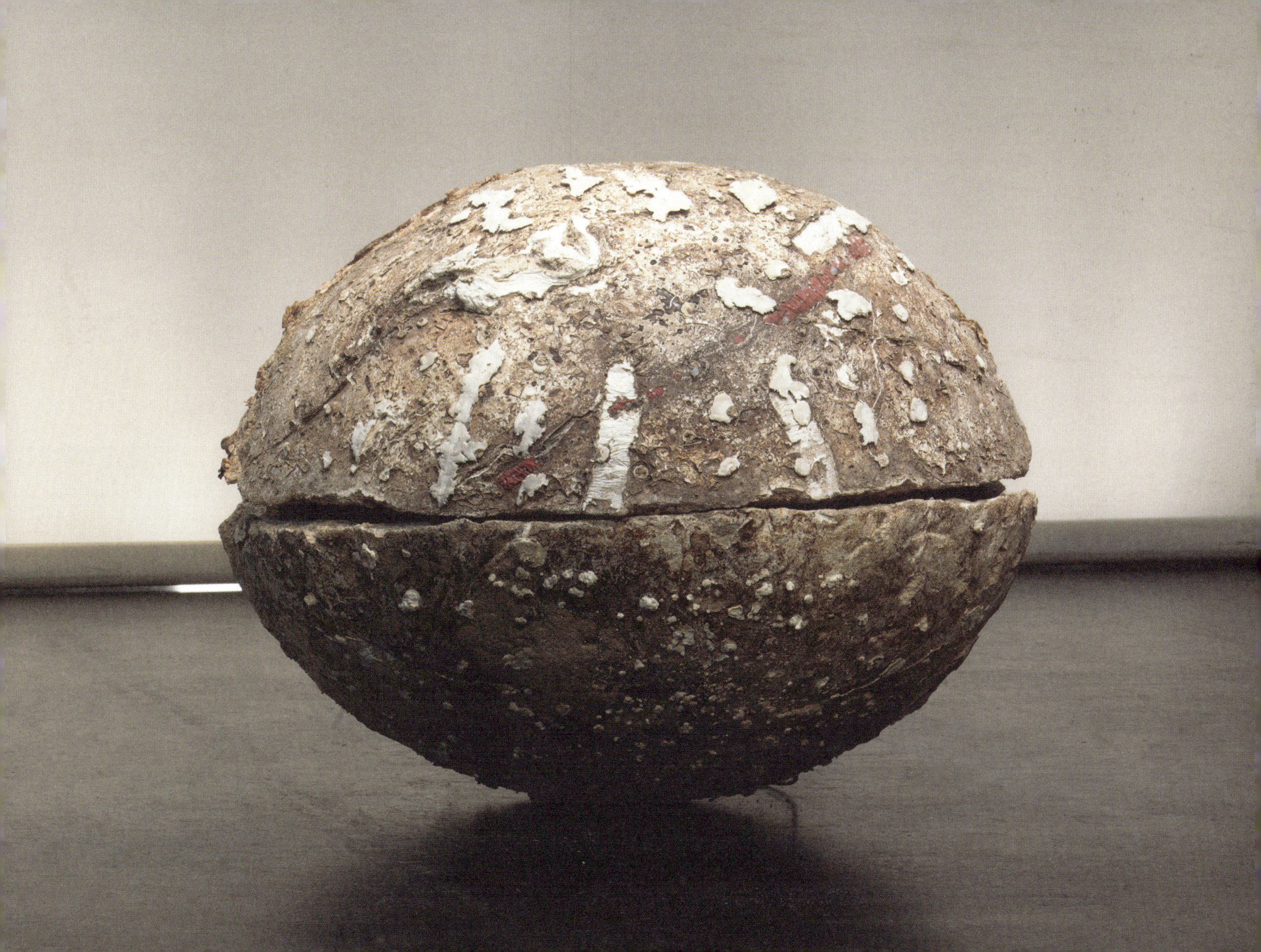

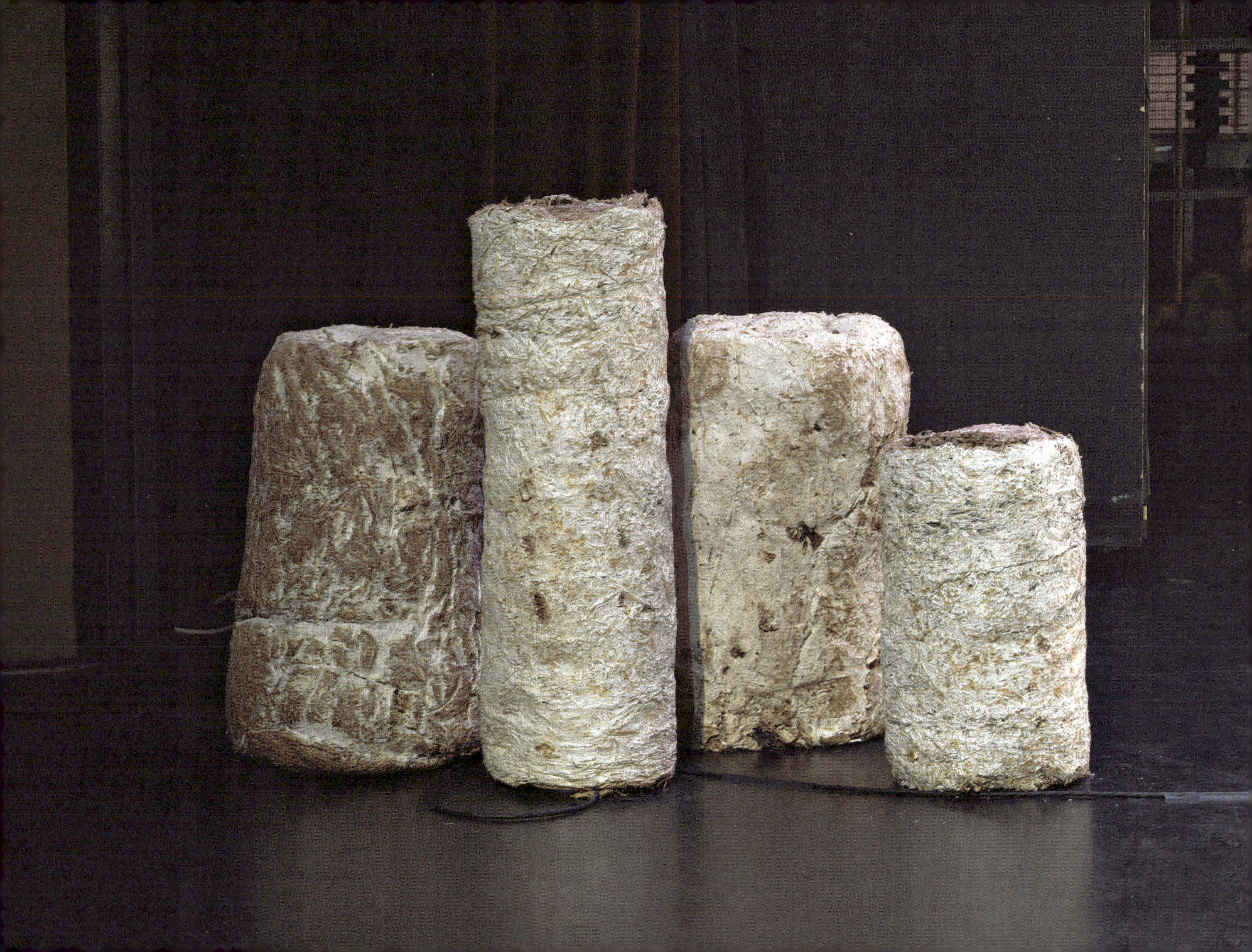

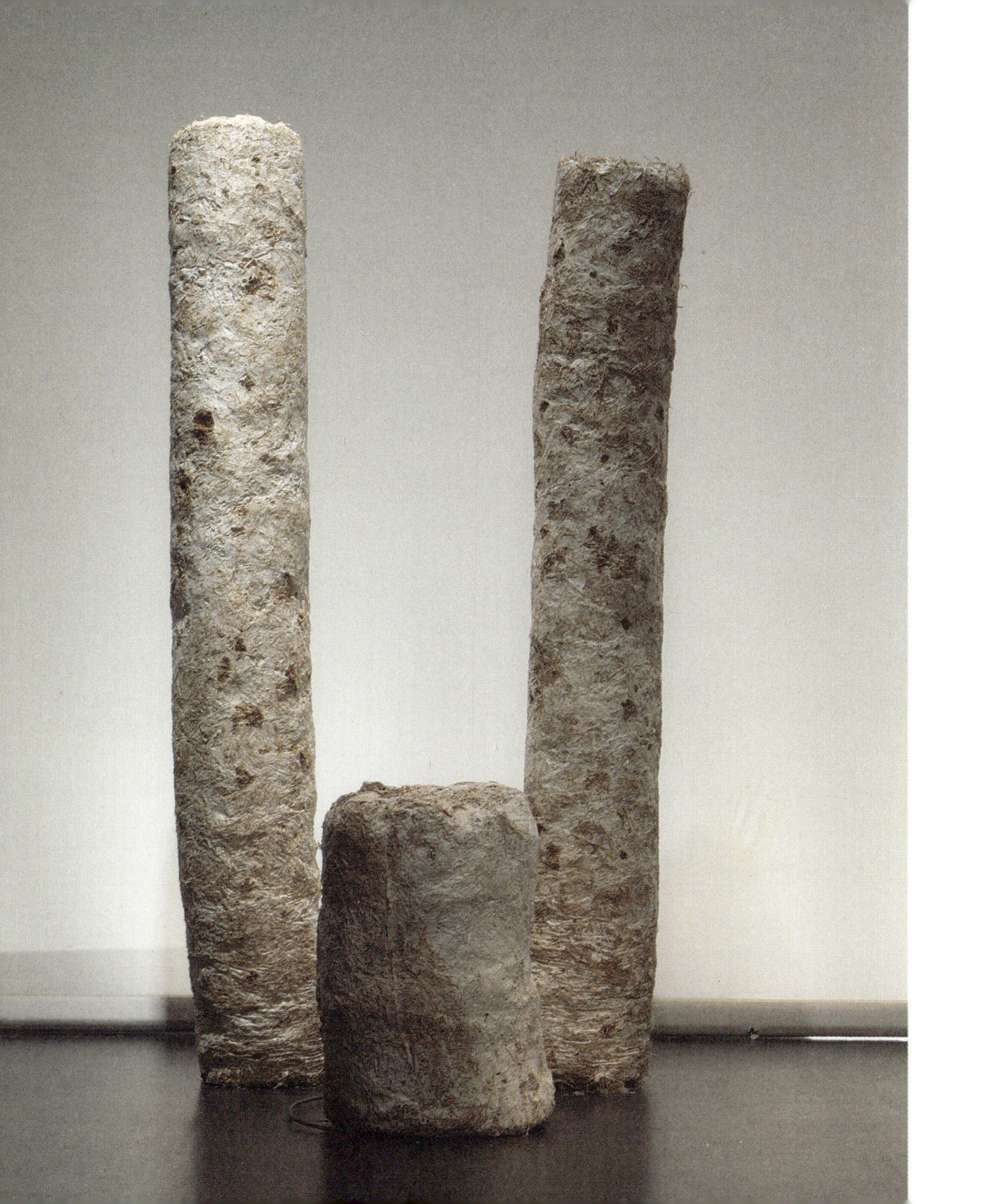

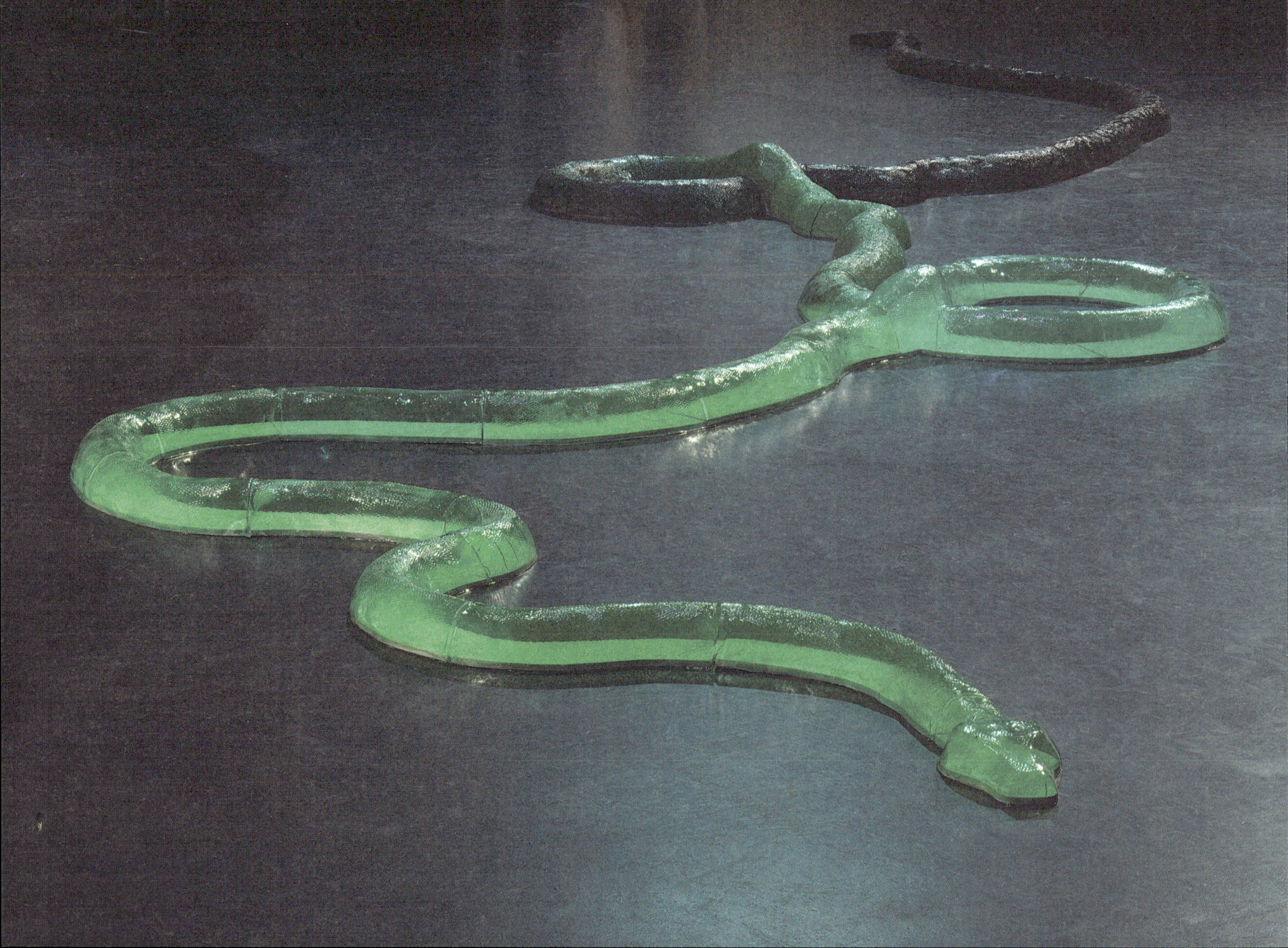

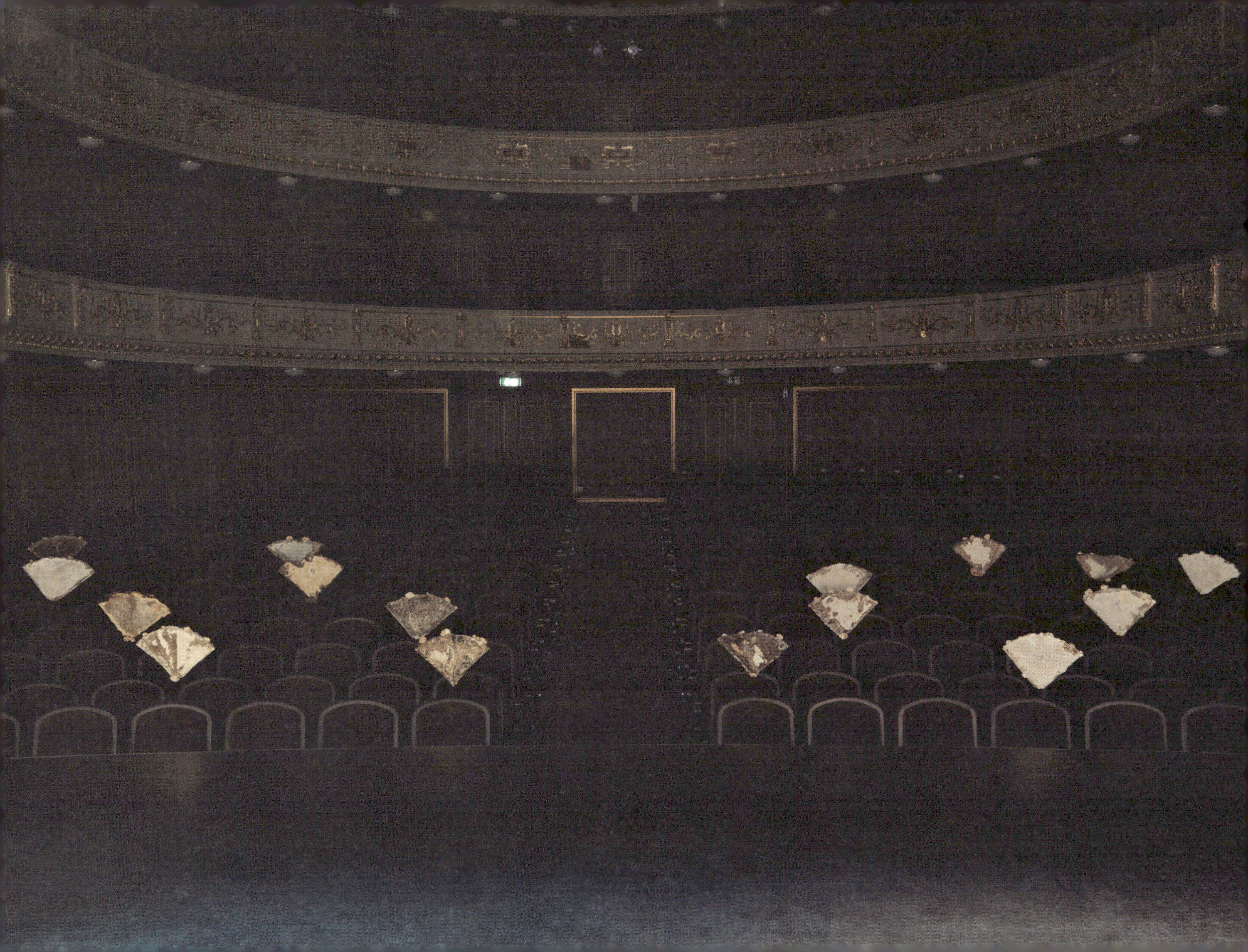

Python

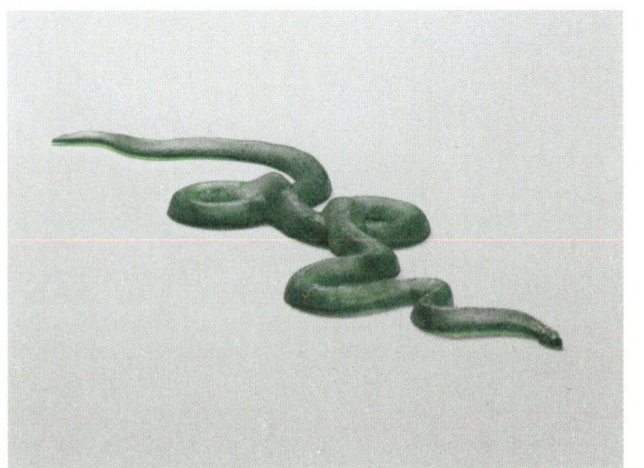

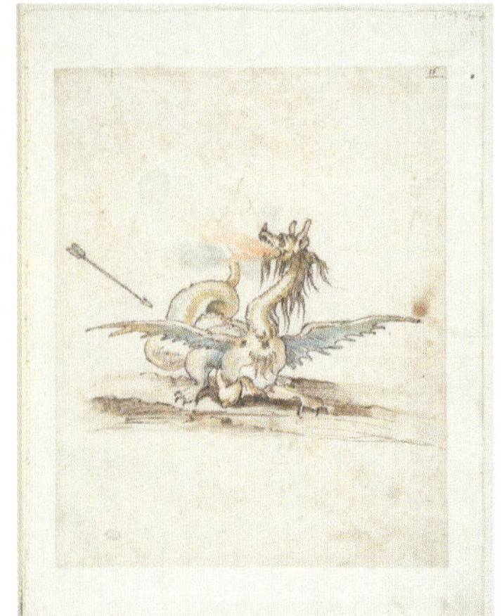

Chorus

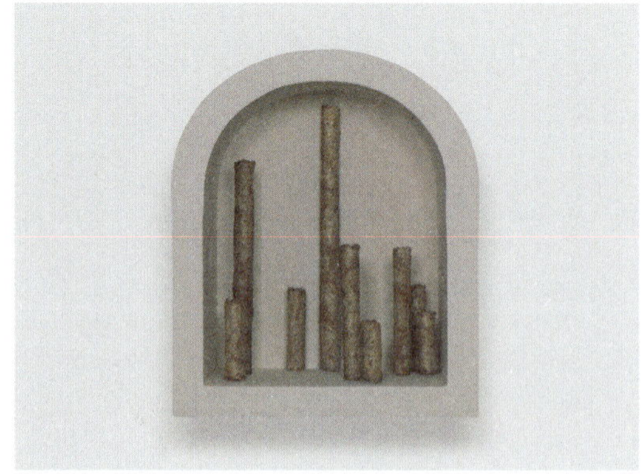

Ovid

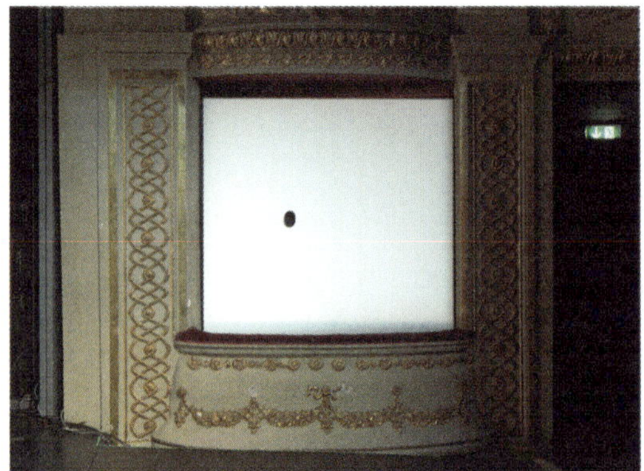

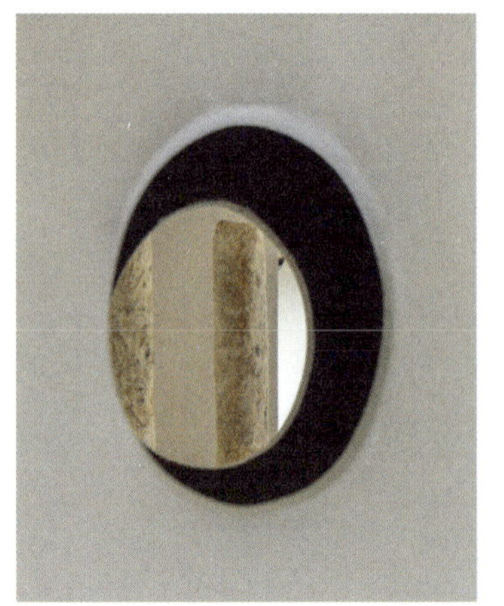

dafne phono libretto 3

Wherein the translations from Libretto 2
are re-translated word for word into Greek.

[Πρόλογος]

Οβίδιος
Από τα μακάρια πεδία, όπου οι αθάνατοι
απολαμβάνουν, στη σκιά της φυλλωσιάς των μυρτιών,
τα ευλογημένα, ευτυχισμένα πνεύματατου Ουρανού,
Εμφανίζομαι μπροστά σας θνητοί απόψε.
Εγώ είμαι εκείνος που στη λύρα του τραγούδησε τα πάθη θεϊκών εραστών,
και τις μεταμορφωμένες μορφές τους,
τόσο γλυκά που ο κόσμος ακόμα με θαυμάζει.
Έπειτα δίδαξα την τέχνη του πώς
η φλόγα της Αγάπης ανάβει σε ένα παγωμένο στήθος,
και πώς η ελευθερία αποκαθίσταται σε μια καρδιά
που μαστίζεται από τις σκληρές και ενοχλητικές φλόγες της Αγάπης.
Τώρα συνεχίζω να ακολουθώ το αρχαίο ύφος,
με σαφές παράδειγμα προσπαθώ να σας δείξω,
Κύριοι και κυρές, πόσο επικίνδυνο είναι
να αντιμετωπίζεις σαν ένα τίποτα τη δύναμη της Αγάπης.
Θα γίνετε μάρτυρες των δακρύων εκείνου του θεού που στον ουρανό φέρει στην ωραία
χρυσή του άμαξα το φως της ημέρας,
και θα τον δείτε να λατρεύει το φωτεινό πνεύμα της αγαπημένης του νύμφης
μέσα στον μεταμορφωμένο κορμό του δέντρου.

[Πρώτο χορικό]

Χορός. *(Ηχώ.)*
Μεθυσμένο με αίμα σε αυτό το σκοτεινό δάσος
μόλις τώρα ξάπλωσε το τρομερό θηρίο. *(Ήταν!)*

[Πρώτο χορικό]

Χορός. *(Ηχώ.)*
Σε αυτό το σκοτεινό δάσος που κείτεται
Μεθυσμένο με αίμα μέχρι θανάτου, άσχημο τέρας.

[Πρόλογος]

Οβίδιος
Η μυθική συμμορία των θεών, που τη σκιάζει η μυρτιά με τα φύλλα της,
Φουσκωμένη με τα πνεύματα των ευλογημένων νεκρών, σμίγει σε μια μακάρια συντροφιά.
Πρόσφατα, από τα πεδία των Ηλυσίων που για σοδειά τους έχουν τη χαρά Ήρθα στα αυτιά σας για να πω, ποιοι είναι γραφτό τους να πεθάνουν.
Εγώ, που τα άγουρα ποιήματά μου, η μαθημένη λύρα τραγούδησε
Ποιες είναι οι αγάπες στον επάνω κόσμο, ποια είναι τα σχήματα που αυτές οι ιερές δυνάμεις αλλάζουν.
Αυτή ήταν η αξία του τραγουδιού μου, τόσο μεγάλη ήταν η διαπεραστική του γλύκα
Αυτή η δόξα στην τέχνη του ποιητή ακόμα δεν με έχει προδώσει.
Εγώ είμαι αυτός που κάποτε δίδαξε την πονηρή φλόγα για να κατακτάς
Καρδιές που δεμένες τις κρατά ο πάγος και πως θα εξευμενιστεί η άγρια μανία
Με την οποία ο έρωτας σκλάβες του κρατά τις καρδιές που χτυπά.
Ούτε τα όπλα της αρχαίας Μούσας το έργο τους δεν σταματούν
Όταν εσύ ακόμα κινδύνους διατρέχεις Ω, άρχοντες και κυρές μου κάτω από τον ζυγό του τυράννου έρωτα:
Που είναι βάρος μου να σας δείξω με το παράδειγμα μιας νότας
Θα ‘πρεπε έστω στο μυαλό σας στην εξουσία τους ελαφρά να φέρεστε.
Θαύματα θα σας φανερωθούν: πώς τα μάτια με τα δάκρυα σκοτεινιάζουν

Χορός. *(Ηχώ)*
Μεθυσμένο με αίμα σε τούτο το σκοτεινό δάσος
τώρα κείτεται το τρομερό θηρίο *(Εκεί ήταν!)*

[Πρώτο]

Πιες το μαύρο αίμα
Για να το σκοτώσεις, τον σκότωσε

Έτσι δεν δηλητηριάζει πια
την υπέροχη εξοχή μας; Έχει πάει αλλού; *(Έφυγε!)*
Αλίμονο, ποιος θα μας υπερασπιστεί αν
το κακό
θηρίο επιστρέψει σήμερα; *(Εγώ!)*
Ποιος είσαι εσύ που μας καθησυχάζεις και μας παρηγορείς; *(Ο Ήλιος!)*
Είσαι ο Ήλιος; Είσαι ο θεός της Δήλου; *(Εγώ!)*
Έχεις το τόξο σου μαζί σου για να τον χτυπήσεις, Απόλλωνα; *(Το έχω!)*
Αν έχεις το τόξο σου, ρίξε μέχρι θανάτου.
σε τού το άσπλαχνο τέρας που μας
κατασπαράζει. *(Τώρα!)*

*Ο Πύθωνας και ο Απόλλωνας
στη σκηνή. Ο Πύθωνας είναι νεκρός*

[Πρώτη σκηνή]

Απόλλων
Ο κακός δράκος κείτεται επιτέλους νεκρός
στην αιματοβαμμένη γη,
σκοτωμένος από το αήττητο τόξο μου.
Πηγαίνετε με ασφάλεια στο λιβάδι,
νύμφες και βοσκοί, πηγαίνετε με ασφάλεια στο δάσος.
Όχι πια φλόγες και δηλητήριο
η φρικτή του ανάσα δε θα μολύνει τους αγνούς ουρανούς.
Αφήστε τα όμορφα τριαντάφυλλα να επιστρέψουν
στα αγαπημένα σας μάγουλα,
η καρδιά σας να είναι εύκολη, το πρόσωπό σας ήρεμο.
Πήρα την ψυχή και την ανάσα από το άσπλαχνο φίδι.

Θα δηλητηρίαζε περισσότερο το αγαπημένο μας χωριό; Μήπως έφυγε και πήγε αλλού;
Αλλά ποιος θα μας προστατεύσει τότε αν το κακό θηρίο επιστρέψει σήμερα;
Ποιος είσαι εσύ που θα μας ηρεμήσεις και θα μας παρηγορήσεις; *(Ο ήλιος!)*
Είσαι ο Ήλιος; Είσαι ο θεός των Δηλίων; *(Εγώ!)*
Έχεις το τόξο για να τον χτυπήσεις, Απόλλωνα; *(Το έχω!)*
Αν έχεις το τόξο, σκότωσε αυτό το άσπλαχνο τέρας που μας κατασπαράζει. *(Τώρα!)*

Άνθρωποι τραγουδούν. *(Αφήνοντας φωνή.)*
Μεθυσμένο και με αίμα σκεπασμένο
μες στο δάσος σωριασμένο εδώ,
Έτσι κείτεται το τέρας τώρα. *(Έτσι κειτόταν και τότε)*
Τώρα δε δίνει άλλο δηλητήριο
Στην τόσο όμορφη εξοχή μας, σε άλλο χωριό αφημένη; *(Αφημένη)*
Αλίμονο, ποιος τώρα θα μας νοιαστεί Αν το τέρας γυρίσει;*(Εγώ!)*
Ποιος είσαι εσύ να μας παρηγορήσεις;
Είσαι εσύ ο θεός Ήλιος;
Είναι ο θεός Δήλος είναι; *(Εγώ!)*
Απόλλων, το τόξο να έχεις μαζί σου και να το λαβώσεις *(Το έχω!)*
Αν τόξο έχεις μαζί σου, σκότωσε πια το τέρας που μεγάλο πόνο σε εμάς προκαλεί. *(Τώρα!)*

ΛΑΤΙΝΙΚΑ ΣΤΑ ΕΛΛΗΝΙΚΑ (ΜΕΣΩ ΑΓΓΛΙΚΩΝ)

Αυτού που έχει τη δύναμη να ανανεώσει την πορεία του
Ήλιου στο άρμα του Και πώς αυτός που χρυσό κομίζει και στη λατρεία ξεχωρίζει, μνηστήρας μιας ημίθεας
Φλερτάρει με το πνεύμα της που πρόσφατα καθηλώθηκε σε ριζωμένο κορμό.

ΣΙΛΜΠΟ (ΙΣΠΑΝΙΚΑ) ΣΕ ΕΛΛΗΝΙΚΑ (ΜΕΣΩ ΑΓΓΛΙΚΩΝ)

Έτσι ώστε να μην δηλητηριάζει
την όμορφη εξοχή μας; Πήγε σε άλλο μέρος; *(Έφυγε!)*
Αλίμονό μας! Ποιος θα μας
υπερασπιστεί αν το κακό θηρίο σήμερα επέστρεφε; *(Εγώ!)*
Ποιος είσαι εσύ που μας δίνεις εμπιστοσύνη και παρηγοριά; *(Ο ήλιος!)*
Είσαι ο ήλιος; Είσαι ο θεός της Δήλου; *(Εγώ!)*
Έχεις το τόξο μαζί σου για να τον λαβώσεις, Απόλλωνα; *(Το έχω!)*
Αν έχεις το τόξο σου, ρίξε μέχρι θανάτου
σε αυτό το σκληρό τέρας που μας καταβροχθίζει. *(Τώρα!)*

ΤΑΑ ΣΤΑ ΕΛΛΗΝΙΚΑ (ΜΕΣΩ ΑΓΓΛΙΚΩΝ)

Με περιγελάς
Στη χώρα μας που έχει ειρήνη και αγάπη;
Πού πηγαίνει; (Έφυγε)
Ποιος θα μας βοηθήσει;
Το φίδι θα μας δαγκώσει (ε μείς)
Ποιος είσαι εσύ που θα μας το πεις; (φίδι)
Εσύ φίδι; Είσαι ο Δήλιος Θεός (ε μείς)
Αυτός έριξε το βέλος; (Ο Απόλλων) ρίχνει
Αυτός που έριξε το βέλος σκοτώθηκε
Είναι ο δολοφόνος (φίδι)

ΙΤΑΛΙΚΑ ΣΕ ΕΛΛΗΝΙΚΑ
(ΜΕΣΩ ΑΓΓΛΙΚΩΝ)

[Δεύτερο χορικό]

Χορός
Θεϊκέ Θεέ, που με το πύρινο άρμα σου
ιππεύεις στον ουρανό,
ντύσε τη μέρα με χρυσό μανδύα.
Αν μέσα σε φρικτές, παγωμένες σκιές
ο ουρανός λάμπει με φως,
δική σου πράγματι είναι η δόξα και περηφάνια.
Αν λουλούδια και φύλλα ανθίσουν,
και τα δάση και τα χωράφια, και
η απέραντη γη ανανεώνει τον ωραίο της μανδύα,
αν με τους γλυκούς της
θησαυρούς κάθε φυτό στολίζεται
δική σου πράγματι είναι η δόξα και περηφάνια.
Μέσα από σένα ζει και
απολαμβάνει το θνητό μάτι ό,τι διακρίνει,
ω κυβερνήτη του αιώνιου άρματος.
Μα όλοι οι άλλοι έπαινοι πρέπει να παραμεριστούν,
μόνο για το τόξο και το βέλος
θα πρέπει να υψωθεί η κραυγή στους υψηλότερους ουρανούς.
Ευγενής έπαινος! Ο περήφανος δράκος,
οπλισμένος με δηλητήριο και με φλόγες,
έχυσε την ψυχή του πάνω στη γη.
Για να πλέξει γιρλάντες και στέμματα
για το όμορφο μέτωπο που είναι γεμάτο ακτίνες,
ποιο είναι το πιο άξιο: η δάφνη ή ο φοίνικας;

ΑΜΠΧΑΖΙΚΑ ΣΕ ΕΛΛΗΝΙΚΑ
(ΜΕΣΩ ΑΓΓΛΙΚΩΝ)

[Δεύτερο χορικό]

Χορός
Ο παντοδύναμος Θεός,
που με το πύρινο άρμα του διασχίζει τον ουρανό,
ντύνει τη μέρα μας με χρυσό μανδύα.
Αν μέσα σε φρικτές, παγωμένες σκιές
ο ουρανός λάμπει με φως,
δικές σου είναι πράγματι η δόξα και η περηφάνια.
Αν φύλλα και λουλούδια ανθίζουν,
και δάση και χωράφια, και
η απέραντη γη ανανεώνει τον ωραίο της μανδύα,
αν στολίζει με θησαυρούς θησαυρούς
κάθε φυτό
δική σου είναι πράγματι η δόξα, η λαμπερή μας περηφάνια.
Ω, εσύ άρχοντα του αθάνατου άρματος
Μέσα από σένα ζει και απολαμβάνει του θανάτου
το μάτι.
Μα όλοι οι άλλοι έπαινοι πρέπει να μείνουν στην άκρη,
μόνο για το τόξο και το βέλος θα πρέπει να υψωθεί
η κραυγή που υψώνεται στους ουρανούς.
Ευγενής έπαινος!
οπλισμένος με δηλητήριο και με φλόγες, του περήφανου δράκου
η ψυχή χύθηκε και έπεσε πάνω στη γη.
Στέμματα πρέπει να πλέκονται...
για το όμορφο μέτωπο που είναι ντυμένο με ακτίνες,
ποιο θα ταίριαζε περισσότερο: να είναι από δάφνη ή φύλλα φοίνικα;

CHATINO ΣΤΑ ΕΛΛΗΝΙΚΑ
(ΜΕΣΩ ΑΓΓΛΙΚΩΝ)

Άνθρωποι τραγουδούν
Ο θεός που είναι μέσα σε μέταλλο που λάμπει
πετάει γλιστρώντας στον ουρανό τη
μέρα στολίζει με λαμπερό πανί
Όταν γίνεται φρίκη, γίνεται φως παγωμένο
ουρανός λάμπει με φως
εσύ πράγματι δόξα περηφάνια.
σαν φύλλα με λουλούδια να το έχουν ανθίσει
και μέσα στο δάσος και τα λιβάδια
και η γη ανανεώνει το μανδύα της και καθένα και θησαυρός γλυκός
και κάθε φυτό στολίζει
εσύ είσαι που δόξα και περηφάνια.
Μέσα από χαρά ήρθες φως γης
όλα διακρίνουν να σπείρουν βράχος πρόσωπο θνητός
ιερός οποίος διατάζει τα πάντα αιώνια
Τα πάντα που δεν είναι έπαινος πρέπει να έχει στο πλάι αφήσει
μόνο τόξο και βέλος που τα χρησιμοποιούν και τόξο μόνο που
πρέπει προσευχές να φωνάζει οι δικές μας στον ουρανό φτάνουν.
Ευγενής έπαινος. Ζώο μεγάλο που φωτιά φτύνει,
οπλισμένο με δηλητήριο και φλόγες,
έχυσε ψυχή στη γη
Γιρλάντες να υφάνουν με πράγμα στο κεφάλι
για ένα στόμα κεφαλιού που ακτίνες κρεμάει
τι ταιριάζει πιο πολύ: δάφνη ή φοίνικας;

Χορός
Θεέ μου θεϊκέ, που με την πύρινη άμαξά σου
περιφέρεσαι σε όλο τον ουρανό,
ντύσε την ημέρα με χρυσό μανδύα.
Αν ανάμεσα στη φρικτή παγωμένη σκιά
ο ουρανός λάμπει με το φως σου,
δικές σου επίσης είναι η δόξα και η υπερηφάνεια.

Αν ανθίζουν φύλλα και λουλούδια,
Δάση και χωράφια, και
ολόκληρη η γη ανανεώνει τον όμορφο μανδύα της,
αν με τους
γλυκούς θησαυρούς,
όλα τα φυτά στολίζουν
δικές σου επίσης είναι η δόξα και η υπερηφάνεια.
Μέσα από εσένα ζει και αγαλλιάζει
Ό,τι αντιλαμβάνεται το θνητό μάτι, ω
κυβερνήτη του αιώνιου άρματος.
Κι όμως, όλοι οι έπαινοι πρέπει να παραμεριστούν,
μόνο το τόξο και το βέλος
αν η κραυγή υψώνεται στους ουρανούς πιο ψηλά.
Ευγενής δόξα! Ο δράκος τιμημένος
οπλισμένος με δηλητήριο και φλόγες,
έχει αδειάσει την ψυχή του στη γη.
Για να πλέξει γιρλάντες και στέμματα
στο όμορφο μέτωπο στολισμένο με αχτίδες,
Ποιο θα είναι πιο άξιο, η δάφνη ή ο φοίνικας;

[Δεύτερο]

Είσαι ο Θεός μας
Από τον ουρανό
Αυτός στόλισε τον κόσμο και τους ουρανούς
Η σκιά είναι πολύ κρύα
Ο κόσμος έχει φως και λάμπει
Ο κόσμος σου με κάνει ευτυχισμένο
Και τα δέντρα παίρνουν λουλούδια και φύλλα
Και τα δέντρα είναι τόσο όμορφα
Και δέντρα στόλισε και φαίνεται όμορφο
Είσαι πράγματι μεγάλος Θεός
Τα πάντα που βλέπουμε ένα άγγιγμα περνάει μέσα
από σένα
Μέσω του Θεού
Ω, εσύ ο πιο υψηλός Θεός
Δεν μας άφησες ποτέ
Ψάχνουμε για Τόξο και Βέλος
Ω είναι ευτυχισμένο
Ας μας προετοίμασε
Εκπνέουμε την ψυχή σου, στον κόσμο
Στόλισε
Τα φρύδια των ματιών του

[Δεύτερη σκηνή]

Έρωτας και Αφροδίτη

Έρωτας
Ότι ψάχνεις για κρίνα ή τριαντάφυλλα
για να στολίσουν τα μαλλιά σου,
Δεν μπορώ να σε πιστέψω, όχι, καλή μητέρα.

Αφροδίτη
Τι ψάχνω τότε, γιε μου;

Έρωτας
Ούτε τριαντάφυλλο ούτε κρίνο:
αναζητάς τον Άδωνι ή κάποιον άλλο πιο όμορφο
ευχάριστο ποιμένα.

Αφροδίτη
Ω, αλίμονο, αλίμονο! Ιδού ο άρχοντας
της Δήλου:
σήμερα όλοι οι θεοί του ουρανού περνούν μέσα από
το δάσος.

Απόλλων, Έρωτας και Αφροδίτη

Απόλλων
Πες μου, πανίσχυρε τοξότη,
ποιο άγριο θηρίο περιμένεις, ή σε ποιο φίδι στήνεις
ενέδρα,
έτσι που κρατάς τη φαρέτρα και το τόξο;

Έρωτας
Ακόμα κι αν ο δράκος
δεν σκοτώθηκε από το τόξο μου,
δεν είμαι ένας τοξότης που αξίζει ακόμη
περιφρόνηση,

[Δεύτερη σκηνή]

Έρωτας και Αφροδίτη

Έρωτας
Κρίνα ή τριαντάφυλλα αναζητάς
για να ομορφύνεις τα μαλλιά σου,
Καλή μητέρα, δεν μπορώ να σε εμπιστευτώ

Αφροδίτη
Τι τότε ψάχνω, γιε μου;

Έρωτας
Ούτε ρόδο ούτε κρίνο:
Τον Άδωνι αναζητάς ή κάποιον άλλον ομορφότερο
κι ευχάριστο ποιμένα.

Αφροδίτη
Ω, αλίμονο, αλίμονο! Ιδού ο άρχοντας της Δήλου:
σήμερα όλοι οι θεοί του ουρανού περνούν μέσα από
το δάσος.

Απόλλων, Έρωτας και Αφροδίτη

Έρωτας
Ακόμα και αν ο δράκος δεν σκοτώθηκε από το τόξο
μου,
δεν είμαι ένας τοξότης που την περιφρόνηση αξίζει,
ο Απόλλωνας είμαι, ένας επουράνιος θεός.

Έρωτας
Ναι, σίγουρα θα το καταλάβεις!

Έρωτας
Ξέρω ότι δεν φοβάσαι τη δύναμη ενός παιδιού,
ω, φονιά των άσχημων τεράτων και φιδιών,

Έρωτας και έναστρο βράδυ

Έρωτας
Πήγαινε να βρεις περισσότερα λουλούδια
τριαντάφυλλα ή ορχιδέες
για να ντύσεις τα μαλλιά σου
Όχι, πίστεψέ με, εσύ, όχι, καλή μητέρα.

Έρωτας
Ούτε λουλούδι τριαντάφυλλο ούτε λουλούδι κρίνα
πας να βρεις τον Άδωνι ή άλλον άντρα όμορφο
είναι
όπως ένας βοσκός που καλά μιλά.

Απόλλωνας, Έρωτας και έναστρο βράδυ

Έρωτας
Ακόμη και ζώο δράκος
δεν πέθανε με τόξο δικό μου,
καλό κάνει τοξότης δεν σας δώσει γέλιο
σε μένα,αλλά εγώ,
ο Απόλλωνας, είμαι ο θεός του ουρανού.

Έρωτας
Ναι, ξέρω σίγουρα

Έρωτας
Ξέρω καλά εγώ δεν φοβάμαι εσσένα
δύναμη του παιδιού
είναι ένα άτομο φονιάς που σκοτώνει τέρατα και
φίδια,
χωρίς σταματημό που περιγελάς και με κοροϊδεύεις.

ΣΙΛΜΠΟ (ΙΣΠΑΝΙΚΑ) ΣΕ ΕΛΛΗΝΙΚΑ (ΜΕΣΩ ΑΓΓΛΙΚΩΝ)

Έρωτας και Αφροδίτη

Έρωτας
Ότι ψάχνεις για κρίνα ή τριαντάφυλλα για να
στολίσεις τα μαλλιά σου
Δεν θέλω να το πιστέψω, όχι, όμορφη μητέρα.

Αφροδίτη
Τότε τι ψάχνω, γιε μου;

Έρωτας
Ούτε τριαντάφυλλο ούτε κρίνο:
ψάχνεις τον Άδωνι να βρεις, ή κάποιον άλλον
ακόμη πιο όμορφο και
γοητευτικό βοσκό.

Αφροδίτη
Ω, για δες εδώ! Καλώς τον άρχοντα της Δήλου:
σήμερα όλοι οι ουράνιοι θεοί περνούν από τα δάση.

Δάφνη, Απόλλων και Έρωτας

Έρωτας
Ακόμη και αν ο δράκος
δεν πέθανε από το τόξο μου
Δεν είμαι ένας τοξότης που ακόμη αξίζει
περιφρόνηση
αλλά και πάλι εγώ, ο Απόλλωνας, είμαι ουράνιος
θεός.

Έρωτας
Ναι, θα το μάθεις με βεβαιότητα!

ΤΑΑ ΣΤΑ ΕΛΛΗΝΙΚΑ (ΜΕΣΩ ΑΓΓΛΙΚΩΝ)

Έρωτας και Αφροδίτη

Έρωτας
Τι ψάχνεις για τριαντάφυλλα
λουλούδια να στολιστείς.. Δεν σε
πιστεύω, χαριτωμένη μου μαμά.

Αφροδίτη
Τι νομίζεις ότι ψάχνω παιδί μου

Έρωτας
Δεν ψάχνεις για τριαντάφυλλα λουλούδια,
ψάχνεις τον Άδωνι να βρεις ή έναν
όμορφο βοσκό ή έναν όμορφο κύριο

Αφροδίτη
Ω, όχι, όχι, είναι ο Θεός της Δήλου.
Σήμερα ο Θεός και ο κόσμος θα
περπατήσουν μέσα από τα δέντρα
Απόλλων, Έρωτας και Αφροδίτη

Έρωτας
Δεν με νοιάζει αν δεν θα
σκοτώσω τον δράκο με το βέλος μου,
αλλά είμαι Έρωτας, είμαι και Θεός

Έρωτας
Ναι, θα ξέρεις ποιος είμαι,
αν και είμαι μικρός, απλώς με
περιγελάς.

Έρωτας
Το ξέρω και πίστεψα ότι είσαι
ηρωίδα και ισχυρή και περιγελάς

αλλά κι εγώ, ο Απόλλωνας, είμαι ουράνιος θεός.

Απόλλων
Αυτό το ξέρω, αλλά όταν τραβάς
το τόξο, αποκαλύπτεις τα μάτια σου, ή
ρίχνεις στα τυφλά, δεινέ τοξότη;

Έρωτας
Ναι, θα το ξέρεις σίγουρα!

Απόλλων
Ω, κάνεις λάθος που θυμώνεις:
Συγχώρεσέ με, Αγάπη,
ή, αν θέλεις να με πληγώσεις, λυπήσου την καρδιά μου.

Έρωτας
Ξέρω καλά ότι δεν φοβάσαι τη δύναμη ενός παιδιού,
ω φονιά τεράτων και φιδιών,
αλλά ακόμη με κοροϊδεύεις και με χλευάζεις.

Αφροδίτη
Θα δεις πόσο μεγάλος κίνδυνος είναι να αστειεύεσαι μαζί του,
κι ας είναι ένα μικρό αγόρι, γυμνό και τυφλό.

[Τρίτο χορικό]

Χορός
Αυτός που ζει απελευθερωμένος από τα δεσμά της αγάπης,
ας απολαύσει την ελευθερία του ευτυχισμένα,
αλλά όχι αλαζονικά: τυλιγμένος σε ένα σκοτεινό σύννεφο
για μας είναι το υψηλό διάταγμα του

αλλά εσύ ακόμα με κοροϊδεύεις και με χλευάζεις.

Αφροδίτη
Θα δεις τι κίνδυνος είναι να αστειεύεσαι μαζί του,
ακόμα κι αν είναι μικρός, γυμνός και τυφλός.

[Τρίτο χορικό]

Χορός
Όποιος ζει απελευθερωμένος από την αγάπη,
ας απολαύσει την ελευθερία του ευτυχισμένα,
αλλά όχι αλαζονικά: τυλιγμένος σε ένα σκοτεινό σύννεφο
με το υψηλό διάταγμα που δείχνουν οι ουρανοί.
Αν δεν έχεις έστω και λίγη Αγάπη,

Άνθρωποι τραγουδούν
Αυτός αχαλίνωτος που δεσμεύει με αγάπη τον κόσμο
σου επιτρέπει που περπατάς ευτυχισμένος μόνος
αλλά όχι αλαζόνας: τυλιγμένος σε σύννεφο σκοτεινό
Για μας ήρθε ουρανός άνοιξε σε εμάς

Έρωτας
Ξέρω καλά ότι δεν φοβάσαι τη δύναμη ενός παιδιού
ω, φόνισσα τεράτων και φιδιών,
κι όμως, με περιγελάς κι αυτό σε διασκεδάζει.

Χορός
Αυτός που ζει χωρίς τις αλυσίδες από της αγάπης
τα δεσμά,
Ας απολαύσει ευτυχισμένα την ελευθερία του,
αλλά όχι περήφανος: τυλιγμένο σε ένα σκοτεινό
σύννεφο
για μας είναι το υψηλό διάταγμα του ουρανού.

μόνο και μόνο επειδή είμαι παιδί και εσύ φόνισσα
μεγάλων
φιδιών και δράκου

Αφροδίτη
Θα δεις τι θα συμβεί
σε σένα, αν και είναι ένα
παιδί θα δεις με τα σωληνωτά μάτια σου

[Τρίτο]

Είναι πολύ χαρούμενος
Τώρα απολαμβάνει την ευτυχισμένη ζωή του
Αλλά ακόμη δεν πιστεύει
Ο Θεός θέλει να κάνουμε έτσι στη Γη
Η αγάπη σου είναι πάντα εκεί
Αύριο και καρδιά ηρεμεί

ουρανού.
Αν τώρα δεν νιώθεις ούτε λίγη ούτε πολλή Αγάπη,
αύριο θα έχεις μια ταραγμένη και ανήσυχη καρδιά,
και θα δεις ότι είναι άσπλαχνος και σκληρός
αφέντης
αυτή η Αγάπη, που τόσο υπεροπτικά περιφρονούσες
πριν.

[Τρίτη σκηνή]

Δάφνη, Απόλλων και Έρωτας

Δάφνη
Από το ελάφι που φεύγει μακριά αυτό
είναι το χνάρι του:
αν μόνο το ίδιο το θηρίο ήταν εδώ κοντά.

Απόλλων
Τι απαλό φως υπέροχων ματιών φτάνει
στην καρδιά μου;
Αγαπημένη νύμφη, τι ψάχνεις τριγύρω να βρεις;

Δάφνη
Ψάχνω αν κάποιο θηρίο
περιπλανιόταν σε αυτό το σκοτεινό δάσος.

Απόλλων
Χωρίς να ρίχνεις τα βέλη σου ή να τραβάς το τόξο
σου,
οργώνοντας κοιλάδες ή βουνά,
μπορείς να πάρεις ένα ευγενές θήραμα με τα
όμορφα μάτια σου.

Δάφνη
Δεν επιθυμώ κανένα άλλο θήραμα, καμία άλλη
απόλαυση

αύριο θα έχεις μια ανήσυχη καρδιά,
και θα βρεις ότι είσαι ο σκληρός
και άσπλαχνος αφέντης
που πάντα περιφρονούσες.

[Τρίτη σκηνή]

Δάφνη, Απόλλων και Έρωτας

Δάφνη
Αυτό το χνάρι
Ανήκει στο φευγαλέο ελάφι
αν μόνο το ίδιο το ζώο ήταν εδώ κοντά.

Δάφνη
Αν κάποιο θηρίο σ' αυτό το σκοτεινό
δάσος
περιπλανιέται, τότε κοιτάζω

Δάφνη
Πέρα από τα άγρια θηρία των δασών και τα δάση
Δεν ξέρω άλλη απόλαυση, τότε αν υπάρχει ένα
περιπλανώμενο ελάφι
και ένα αγριογούρουνο που μπορώ να σκοτώσω,
άλλη απόλαυση δεν έχω.

Δάφνη
Εκτός από το βέλος μου,
δεν θέλω κανέναν σύντροφο, αντίο.

Έρωτας
Δες, πώς κατάφερα να σε παγιδεύσω.
Ω, μάθε τι σημαίνει να περιφρονείς την ηλικία μου

τώρα με λύπη περισσότερο σε νιώθει αύριο
ταραγμένη και ανήσυχη καρδιά δική σου είναι.
Θα αναρωτιέσαι επειδή είναι ένας αφέντης άκαρδος
και σκληρός
που αγάπη, την οποία δίνει υπεροπτικά έχει
περιφρονήσει εσένα παλιά.

Δάφνη, Απόλλωνας και Έρωτας

Δάφνη
Από στο ελάφι που φυγάς
είναι ότι εδώ αχνάρι
αν περιπλανώμενο ζώο που κοντά εδώ.

Δάφνη
Κοιτάζοντας εγώ αν κάποιο ζώο
περιπλανώμενο μέσα δάσος σκοτεινό αυτό.

Δάφνη
Δεν θέλω εγώ άλλο θήραμα, ούτε άλλο πράγμα
απόλαυση
ζώο άγριο και μέσα σε δάσος,
ευχαριστημένη και ευτυχής εγώ.
Αν ρίξω σε ελάφι που τρέχει ή ρίξω σε
αγριογούρουνο

Δάφνη
με τόξο αυτό δικό μου,
δεν χρειάζεται άλλος σύντροφος να έρθει μαζί μου,
εγώ φεύγω.

Έρωτας
ήδη είδες τώρα? Ένιωσα εσένα μέσα παγίδα.

Αν τώρα δεν νιώθεις ούτε λίγη ούτε πολλή αγάπη,
αύριο θα έχεις καρδιά
ταραγμένη και ανήσυχη,
και θα δεις ότι ο ιδιοκτήτης είναι σκληρός
και αυστηρός
είναι η Αγάπη, που πριν την υποτίμησες
τόσο υπερήφανα.

Δάφνη, Απόλλων και Έρωτας

Δάφνη
Του φευγαλέου ελαφιού,
αυτό είναι το ίχνος από το ίδιο χνάρι:
αν μόνο το ίδιο ζώο ήταν κοντά.

Δάφνη
Κοιτώ αν κάποιο ζώο
περιπλανιέται σε τούτο το σκοτεινό δάσος.

Δάφνη
Δεν λαχταρώ άλλο θήραμα, άλλη απόλαυση
πιο πολύ από τα άγρια ζώα και τα δάση,
και χαίρομαι και ευτυχώ
να ρίχνω βέλος σε περιπλανώμενο ελάφι ή
αγριογούρουνο.

Δάφνη
Πέρα από το βέλος μου,
Δεν θέλω παρέα, μέχρι για πάντα.

Η αγάπη, αρχηγέ, η αγάπη είναι τα πάντα

Δάφνη, Απόλλων και Έρωτας

Δάφνη
Το χνάρι της άνοιξης
που είναι εδώ, και θέλω να είναι εδώ τώρα

Δάφνη
Ψάχνω για ζώα αλλά
Δεν έχω ιδέα πού
Έχει πάει

Δάφνη
Αλλά δεν ψάχνω να βρω ένα άλλο
Ζώο, αλλά θα χαρώ πολύ
Αν σκοτώσω χοίρο των θάμνων ή άλλο
Ζώο

Δάφνη
Εγώ και το τόξο και το βέλος μου
θα είμαστε μια χαρά
Δεν θέλουμε να είμαστε με κάποιον

Έρωτας
Από εδώ και πέρα θα πρέπει να
ξέρεις ότι εγώ και το
τόξο μου και το βέλος είμαστε μικρά, αλλά

ΙΤΑΛΙΚΑ ΣΕ ΕΛΛΗΝΙΚΑ (ΜΕΣΩ ΑΓΓΛΙΚΩΝ)	ΑΜΠΧΑΖΙΚΑ ΣΕ ΕΛΛΗΝΙΚΑ (ΜΕΣΩ ΑΓΓΛΙΚΩΝ)	CHATINO ΣΤΑ ΕΛΛΗΝΙΚΑ (ΜΕΣΩ ΑΓΓΛΙΚΩΝ)
πέρα από τα άγρια θηρία και τα δάση, και είμαι ευχαριστημένη και ευτυχής αν ρίξω σε ένα περιπλανώμενο ελάφι ή σε αγριογούρουνο. *Απόλλων* Κι εγώ μπορώ να τραβήξω το τόξο, και αν αυτό δεν σε δυσαρεστεί, ας συμφωνήσουμε να έχουμε ένα υπέροχο κυνήγι μαζί. *Δάφνη* Εκτός από το βέλος μου, δεν θέλω κανέναν σύντροφο, αντίο. *Απόλλων* Αλίμονο, μην είσαι τόσο βιαστικός: Περίμενε, νύμφη, περίμενε. *Έρως* Δες, πώς κατάφερα να σε παγιδεύσω. Ω, μάθε τι σημαίνει να περιφρονείς την ηλικία μου και να υποκλίνεσαι!	και να υποκλίνεσαι!	Ω, ήδη είδα πράγμα συμβαίνει γιατί δίνει αστείο εσύ μεγάλη και τόξο
[Τέταρτο χορικό]	[Τέταρτο χορικό]	
Χορός Τι νέο θαύμα έχουν τα μάτια μου δει! Μέσα σε φυλλωσιές σαν δέντρα ξανθά μαλλιά έχουν γίνει, και το πόδι που μόλις τώρα έτρεξε γρήγορα, θαμμένα στο έδαφος βλασταίνοντας κλαδιά και φύλλα Ίσως ως απάντηση στους αγνούς πόθους η ιερή θεά (Άρτεμις) – αφού η φυγή ήταν μάταιη –	*Χορός* Τι νέο θαύμα έχουν τα μάτια μου δει! Σε φυλλωσιές που μοιάζουν με δέντρα ξανθά μαλλιά μεταμορφώθηκαν, και το πόδι που μόλις τώρα έτρεξε γοργά, θαμμένο στο έδαφος, βλασταίνοντας κλαδιά και φύλλα Ίσως η ιερή θεά (Άρτεμις) Ως απάντηση σε αγνές επιθυμίες – αφού η φυγή	*Άνθρωποι τραγουδούν* Αγαπημένο όμορφο πιο πολύ μοιάζει αυτό είδα σπόρο βράχο πρόσωπο αυτό, σε φύλλα δέντρο πράσινα κρεμασμένα μαλλιά ξανθιά κεφάλι. Και χαλαρό γρήγορο πόδι έτρεξε θαμμένο μέσα στο χώμα βλασταίνει πράγμα κλαδιά και φύλλα. Ίσως ως απάντηση, επειδή αγνές επιθυμίες...

είμαστε ήρωες.

[Τέταρτο]

Χορός
Τι νέο θαύμα
είδαν τα μάτια μου! Σε φύλλα που μοιάζουν δέντρα
τα μαλλιά ξανθά έχουν γίνει,
και το πόδι που μόλις έτρεξε γοργά και ελεύθερα,
θαμμένο στο έδαφος,
βγάζει κλαδιά και φύλλα...
Ίσως ως απάντηση στις διαυγείς επιθυμίες
η ιερή θεά [Άρτεμις] – αφού
το φευγιό ήταν μάταιο –

Όσα είναι όμορφα
Που έχω δει με τα μάτια μου
Το δέντρο που το τρίχωμά του μεταμορφώθηκε σε λευκά φύλλα
Τα χνάρια που τρέχουν τώρα
Εξαφανίστηκε
Και βγάζουν ρίζες και κλαδιά
Ίσως ήθελε μόνο να παραμείνει παρθένα
Η θεά της (Άρτεμις)

προσέφερε τέτοια βοήθεια
όχι ως τιμωρία, όχι, αλλά από έλεος
άλλαξε μια τόσο όμορφη ψυχή σε νέο θάμνο.

[Τέταρτη σκηνή]

Απόλλων
Έτσι αυτός ο τραχύς φλοιός για πάντα
θα περικλείει την παραδεισένια ομορφιά της;
Μάτια, εσείς που είδατε
τη θεσπέσια ομορφιά που σας αναγκάζει να κλαίτε,
κοιτάξτε επίσης αυτά τα κλαδιά,
εδώ βρίσκεται και εδώ κρύβεται
η αγάπη μου, η καρδιά μου, ο θησαυρός μου,
για τον οποίο, αν και αθάνατος, μαραζώνω και
πεθαίνω.
Καταφρονητική και ντροπαλή νύμφη,
που, φεύγοντας μακριά από τον έρωτα ενός
ουράνιου θεού,
άλλαξες την όμορφη μορφή σου σε μια πράσινη
δάφνη,
ποτέ μη γίνει εγώ να μην σε τιμώ και σε αγαπώ
γιατί πάντα στο χρυσό μου μέτωπο τα
φύλλα και τα κλαδιά σου θα φτιάχνουν μια
γιρλάντα.
Αλλά, ω, αν μέσα σε αυτά τα κλαδιά
ακούσεις το κλάμα μου, ακούσεις την αρχοντική
λύρα μου,
και τι δώρα ζητάει για σένα από τον ουρανό.
Ας μη φοβάται το δέντρο μου ούτε τη φωτιά ούτε
τον παγετό,
και ας είναι η αιώνια φορεσιά του από λαμπερό
σμαράγδι,
ούτε η οργή του ουρανού δεν θα το βλάψει ποτέ
ξανά.

ήταν μάταιη
όπως ήταν κατανοητό – πρόσφερε τέτοια βοήθεια,
όχι ως τιμωρία, όχι, αλλά από έλεος άλλαξε μια
τόσο όμορφη ψυχή σε φυτό.

που είναι η θεά [Άρτεμις] - μάταια απογειώθηκε
πρόσφερε βοήθεια σε
καμία τιμωρία, όχι, είναι επειδή το έλεος...
άλλαξε όμορφη ψυχή και άλλον θάμνο πράσινο;

προσέφερε τέτοια βοήθεια,
όχι ως τιμωρία, όχι, αλλά από έλεος
μεταμόρφωσε μια όμορφη ψυχή σε θάμνο.

Της δίνει δύναμη, σθένος να παραμείνει έτσι
Δεν είμαι, όχι, είμαι λυπημένος.
Αλλά η υπέροχη ψυχή της μεταμορφώνεται σε
δέντρο

Οι ωραίοι κύκνοι της Δίρκης και οι άρχοντες που
κυβερνούν
να φέρουν στα φημισμένα μέτωπά τους
ως ένδειξη τιμής γιρλάντες και στεφάνια από τα
πράσινα κλωνάρια του.
Ποτέ ο βοσκός ούτε το κοπάδι του μη βαρεθεί τον
πράσινο μανδύα σου, και μη σε
ξεγυμνώσει και σου τον κλέψει:
Στη φιλόξενη σκιά του, νύμφες και θεές,
χαρούμενα να τραγουδούν, και να περνούν τη
χαρούμενη και εύθυμη μέρα.

[Πέμπτο χορικό]

Χορός
Όμορφη νύμφη που τρέχεις μακριά,
και έχεις πετάξει
την αρχοντική, θνητή μορφή σου,
να χάρεις, νεαρό δέντρο,
αγνό και όμορφο,
αγαπημένο στον κόσμο και αγαπημένο στον
ουρανό.
Δεν ανησυχείς για σύννεφα καταιγίδας ή κεραυνό,
στεφανώνεις
κύκνους, βασιλιάδες και ουράνιους θεούς
είτε ο ουρανός παγώνει, είτε φλέγεται και ζεσταίνει
με σμαράγδια,
χαρούμενα ντύνεσαι και στολίζεσαι.
Κι έτσι, να χαρείς τόσο διακεκριμένα ενδύματα,
τις αρετές σου
δεν ζηλεύω ούτε επιθυμώ.
Γιατί αν ποτέ χτυπηθώ από της Αγάπης
το χρυσό βέλος,
δεν θα πάω σε πόλεμο με θεό.
Αν ποτέ κουνήσω τα πόδια μου για να ξεφύγω

[Πέμπτο χορικό]

Χορός
Όμορφη νύμφη που τρέχεις μακριά,
και έχεις πετάξει την αρχοντική, θνητή μορφή σου,
να χάρεις
αγνό και όμορφο νεαρό δέντρο,
που ταιριάζει με τον κόσμο και τον ουρανό.
Σύννεφα καταιγίδας ή κεραυνό,
Να μη φοβάσαι
τα στεφανώνεις (δίνεις τη βασιλεία τους)
κύκνοι, βασιλιάδες και ουράνιοι θεοί,
είτε ο ουρανός παγώνει, είτε φλέγεται αρκετά για
να σε ζεστάνει ό,τι κι αν συμβαίνει,
χαρούμενα στολίζεσαι με όμορφο φουστάνι
και σμαράγδια (με πράσινα πετράδια).
Να απολαύσεις
τις διακεκριμμένες αρετές σου (σεβασμός/αξία)
Δεν επιθυμώ με φθόνο.
Γιατί αν ποτέ χτυπηθώ από το βέλος της αγάπης,
δεν θα κάνω πόλεμο σε έναν θεό.
Αν αντιπαθώντας την αγάπη και ανελέητος,
σε έναν αληθινό δικό μου εραστή,
αν κινήσω τα πόδια μου για να φύγω μακριά
είθε τα χρυσά μαλλιά μου

Άν θρωποι τραγουδούν
Όμορφη, νύμφη που κρύφτηκε
ελευθέρωσε και έγδυσε αυτούς σε καλή
καρδιά δική σου, επειδή είσαι θνητός
Δέντρο νέο, δέντρο βρέφος στέκεται μόνο,
αγνή εσύ, όμορφη
αγαπημένο, ο κόσμος και ο παράδεισος.
μην ανησυχείς εσύ για σύννεφα που κρέμονται
σκοτεινά και κεραυνός
μέτωπο κάθεται εσύ κεφάλι
πουλί κύκνος, βασιλιάς και ιερός πατέρας
Αν παγώσει ή ζεσταθεί ουρανός με φλόγες
με πετράδι πράσινο πολύτιμο
κάθε μέρα χαρούμενο καλό ύφασμα και να
στολιστείς
δίνει μεγαλύτερη χαρά εσένα με τα πάντα
και δύναμη έχεις εσύ
μη θέλεις και μη ζηλεύεις εμένα με αυτό
Έρθει μέρα θέλεις αγάπη
τόξο χρυσό
δεν πάει πολεμήσει με ιερό δικό μας θεό.
Αν κουνήσω πόδια επειδή τρέξω ελευθερωθώ
ένας άνθρωπος που θέλει αληθινά σε μένα

Χορός

Όμορφη νύμφη που δραπέτευσες
ελεύθερη και απογυμνωμένη
από την αρχοντική σου μορφή θνητή,
να χαίρεσαι, νεαρό δέντρο,
αγνό και όμορφο
αγαπημένο από τον κόσμο και αγαπημένο από τον ουρανό.
Δεν ανησυχείς για τα σύννεφα της καταιγίδας ή του κεραυνού,
στεφανώνεις
κύκνους, βασιλιάδες και θεούς ουράνιους,
αν ο ουρανός παγώσει ή τυλιχτεί στις φλόγες
και θερμανθεί,
με σμαράγδια
στολίσου και ντύσου ευτυχισμένη πάντα.
Να απολαύσεις τις διακρίσεις σου,
τις αρετές σου
που ούτε φθονώ ούτε ποθώ.
Γιατί αν εκπλαγώ με Αγάπη
με το χρυσό του βέλος,
δεν θα πολεμήσω με θεό.
Αν κουνήσω τα ποδιά μου για να

[Πέμπτο]

Η όμορφη κοπέλα τρέχει
Είναι ευτυχισμένη και όχι θλιμμένη
Γιατί είναι μια γυναίκα που είναι
Είναι ευτυχισμένη
Η ομορφιά της με κάνει ευτυχισμένο
Ο κόσμος και η Γη σε αγαπούν
Δεν ανησυχείς για τους κεραυνούς και τα σύννεφα
Τη στεφανώνει μόνο για να δείξει αγάπη
Περιστέρι, αρχηγοί και ο ουράνιος Θεός
Δεν την νοιάζει ο κόσμος και η σκληρότητά του
Με τα μαύρα διαμάντια
Κάθε μέρα γίνεσαι ευτυχισμένη γιατί αφήνεις τη ζωή σου
Νερό με ομορφιά
Με τον όμορφο τρόπο σου
Δεν ζηλεύω αυτό που κάνεις.
Ακόμη κι αν με χτυπήσεις
Με το βέλος που πέφτει
Δεν αναμετριέμαι με τον Θεό
Δεν θα τρέξω
Ποτέ δεν καταλαβαίνεις πόση λύπη έχω
Με τα στολισμένα μου μαλλιά

ΙΤΑΛΙΚΑ ΣΕ ΕΛΛΗΝΙΚΑ
(ΜΕΣΩ ΑΓΓΛΙΚΩΝ)

από αληθινό εραστή,
περήφανο και άσπλαχνο απέναντι στην Αγάπη,
τα χρυσά μαλλιά μου να γίνουν
όχι σαν δάφνη,
αλλά, μάλλον, ισχνό χορτάρι.
Τα ξανθά μαλλιά μου ας γίνουν μικροί μίσχοι
που το αδηφάγο
κοπάδι πάντα διαλύει και σκορπά,
ας είναι χαμηλός σανός που τα άγρια δόντια
των κοπαδιών τα τραβάει η λαίμαργη πείνα.
Αλλά αν για απάντηση σε έναν αναστεναγμό,
ερωτικές παρακλήσεις,
λάμπω και καίγομαι από οίκτο,
αν υπόσχομαι σε αλλού
το μαρτύριο γλυκιά ελπίδα
με χαμόγελο και μια
ματιά,
μην επιτρέψεις, Αγάπη όλο χάρη,
τη θέρμη μου
μάταια να πάρει μια ψυχρή καρδιά,
μην επιτρέψεις σε μια παραλία ή σε ακτή
μια άπιστη καρδιά
να με εγκαταλείψει όταν έχω ερωτευτεί.
Φρόντισε η φωτιά των ματιών μου
να μαλακώσει
κάθε ψυχρότητα, κάθε σκληράδα,
αυτή η καρδιά να καίει τότε ώστε
ένας άλλος να λατρεύει,
όποιος κι
αν είναι, ομορφιά μου.

Τέλος

ΑΜΠΧΑΖΙΚΑ ΣΕ ΕΛΛΗΝΙΚΑ
(ΜΕΣΩ ΑΓΓΛΙΚΩΝ)

να γίνουν όχι σαν δάφνη
αλλά σαν ισχνό χορτάρι.
Είθε τα ξανθά μαλλιά μου να γίνουν ταπεινοί μίσχοι
που το αδηφάγο
κοπάδι πάντα διαλύεται και σκορπίζει γύρω μου,
ας γίνουν ταπεινά άχυρα όπου αγέλες με βάναυσα
δόντια
έλκονται από την άπληστη πείνα.
Αλλά αν για απάντηση σε έναν αναστεναγμό,
ερωτικές παρακλήσεις,
λάμπω και καίγομαι από οίκτο,
αν υπόσχομαι σε αλλού το μαρτύριο
γλυκιά ελπίδα με χαμόγελο και μια ματιά,
μην επιτρέψεις, Αγάπη όλο χάρη,
τη θερμή μου μάταια να πάρει μια ψυχρή καρδιά,
μην επιτρέψεις σε μια παραλία ή σε ακτή
μια άπιστη καρδιά
να με εγκαταλείψει όταν έχω ερωτευτεί.
Φρόντισε η φωτιά των ματιών μου να
μαλακώσει
κάθε ψυχρότητα, κάθε σκληρότητα,
Άφησε αυτή την καρδιά
να καίει τότε
όποιος κι αν είναι,
ομορφιά μου.

CHATINO ΣΤΑ ΕΛΛΗΝΙΚΑ
(ΜΕΣΩ ΑΓΓΛΙΚΩΝ)

δυνατά και μεγάλα κάνει σε μένα για πράγματα που
αγαπώ
χρυσά γίνονται άκουσε κεφάλι μου
όχι είναι λουλούδι δάφνη
αλλά, πολύ καλύτερο αν γίνει γρασίδι ισχνό
ίσως μαλλιά ξανθά το κεφάλι μου γίνει βλαστός
δέντρο σκιά
που ζώο αδηφάγο
όλα τα ζώα τσακίζει οικεία και σκορπίζει γύρω
ας είναι είναι σανός σε βράχο δόντια
ζώο πεινασμένο
ζώο κακό και πεινασμένο
Είναι πράγμα αναστεναγμός αυτούς
είναι παρακλήσεις καλές
λάμψη είναι στέκομαι και προσέχω όλο το καλό
πήρα μια υπόσχεση και έβαλα ένα πράγμα,
να έρθει καλό μόνο
χαρούμενο πρόσωπο και βλέμμα καμιά
άδεια, όλα αγάπη
που δίνει φλόγα στην καρδιά μου
θα έρθει έχει μια καρδιά κρύα για μην
αφήνεις αυτό το στόμα ωκεανό μια
καρδιά που καραδοκεί και αστειεύεται
όχι εγκαταλείπεις εμένα όταν πιο ευτυχής εγώ
βλέπω σε να
επιτρέπει αυτή την ελαφρά φωτιά να δει πρόσωπο
μαλακωμένη είναι
παντού ψυχρότητα, παντού σκληρότητα,
δώσε περισσότερα που καίνε καρδιά
ώστε άλλος τότε να λατρέψεις όποιος κι
αν είναι, ομορφιά μου.

ξεφύγω από έναν αληθινό εραστή,
περήφανου και σκληρού απέναντι στην Αγάπη,
που τα μαλλιά μου ξανθά δεν γίνονται σαν μια δάφνη
αλλά, μάλλον, χορτάρι ασώματο.
Αλλά αν για απάντηση σε έναν αναστεναγμό,
και ερωτικές παρακλήσεις,
λάμπω και καίω με έλεος,
αν υποσχεθώ το μαρτύριο των άλλων γλυκιά ελπίδα
με ένα χαμόγελο και ένα βλέμμα,
μην επιτρέψεις, ευγενική Αγάπη,
το κάψιμό μου
να πάρει μάταια μια παγωμένη ψυχή,
μην επιτρέψεις παράλια ή ακτή
μια καρδιά χωρίς πίστη
να με εγκαταλείψει στην αγάπη
Κάνε τη φωτιά των ματιών μου
να μαλακώσει Όποια ψυχρότητα, όποια σκληρότητα,
Άφησε την καρδιά να καεί
άλλη να τον λατρέψει
όποια κι αν είσαι, ομορφιά μου.

Αυτά είναι τα μαλλιά μου
Αλλά μοιάζουν με χορτάρι που το έχουν σκορπιστεί
Με κοντές τρίχες
Πεινούσες τόσο
Σαν τα ζώα που έχουν μείνει καιρό χωρίς να φάνε
Δεν πεινάει.
Είναι νεκρό
Με τροφή
Είναι πιο ενθουσιασμένη
Με την αγάπη μου παρακαλώ
Ένιωσα να σε έχω ερωτευτεί
Πίστεψα σε σένα
Έχω ενθουσιαστεί
Με ένα χαμόγελο
Με ραγισμένη καρδιά και αγάπη Έχω αγάπη
Δεν νοιάζεται για μένα
Και πρέπει να με πας στην παραλία
Μη με αφήνεις, σε έχω ερωτευτεί
Με τη φωτιά που είναι στα μάτια μου
Η καρδιά μου καίγεται από αγάπη, γιατί η αγάπη που έχω με τους ανθρώπους, αλλά ποιον αγαπώ (ομορφιά μου)

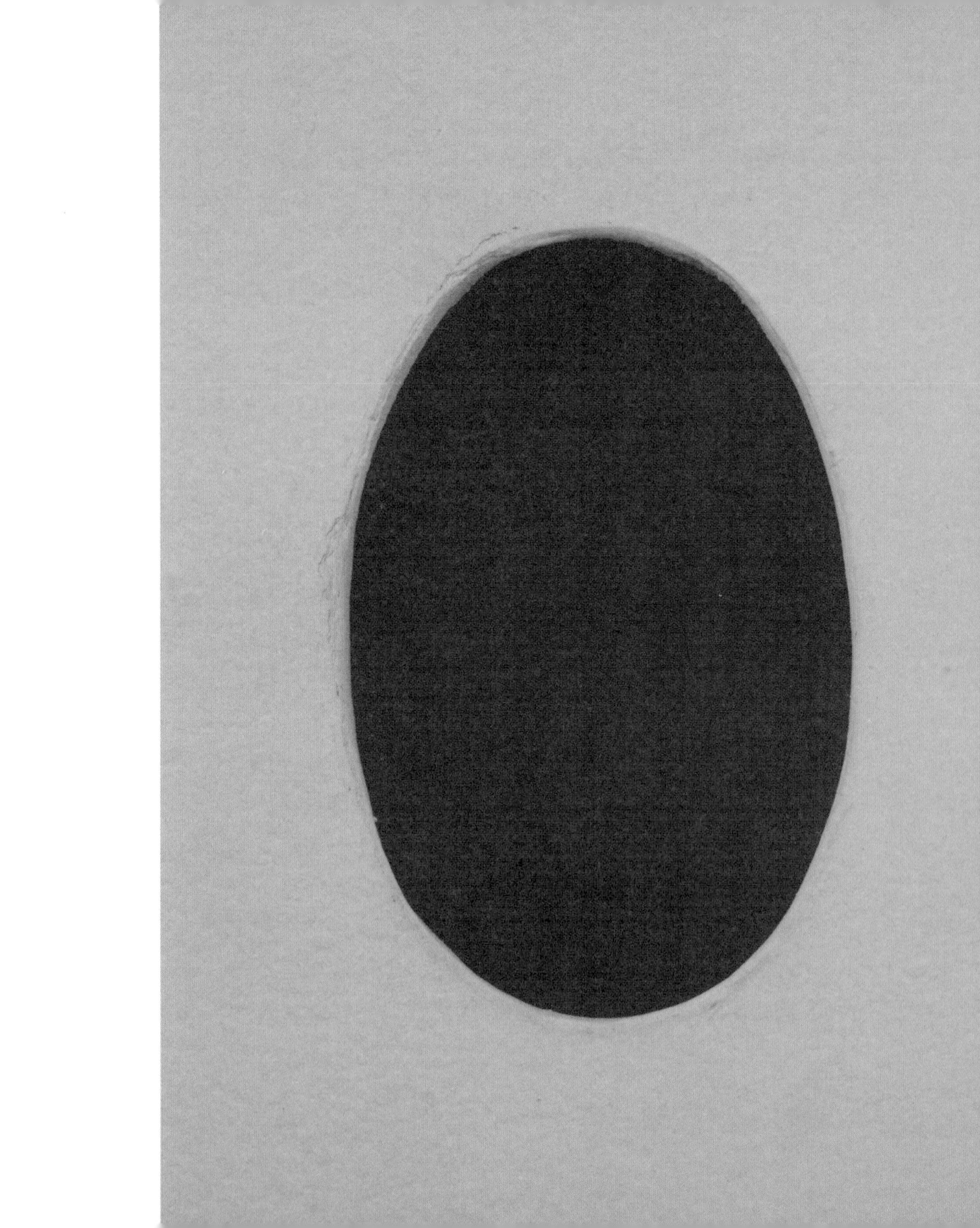

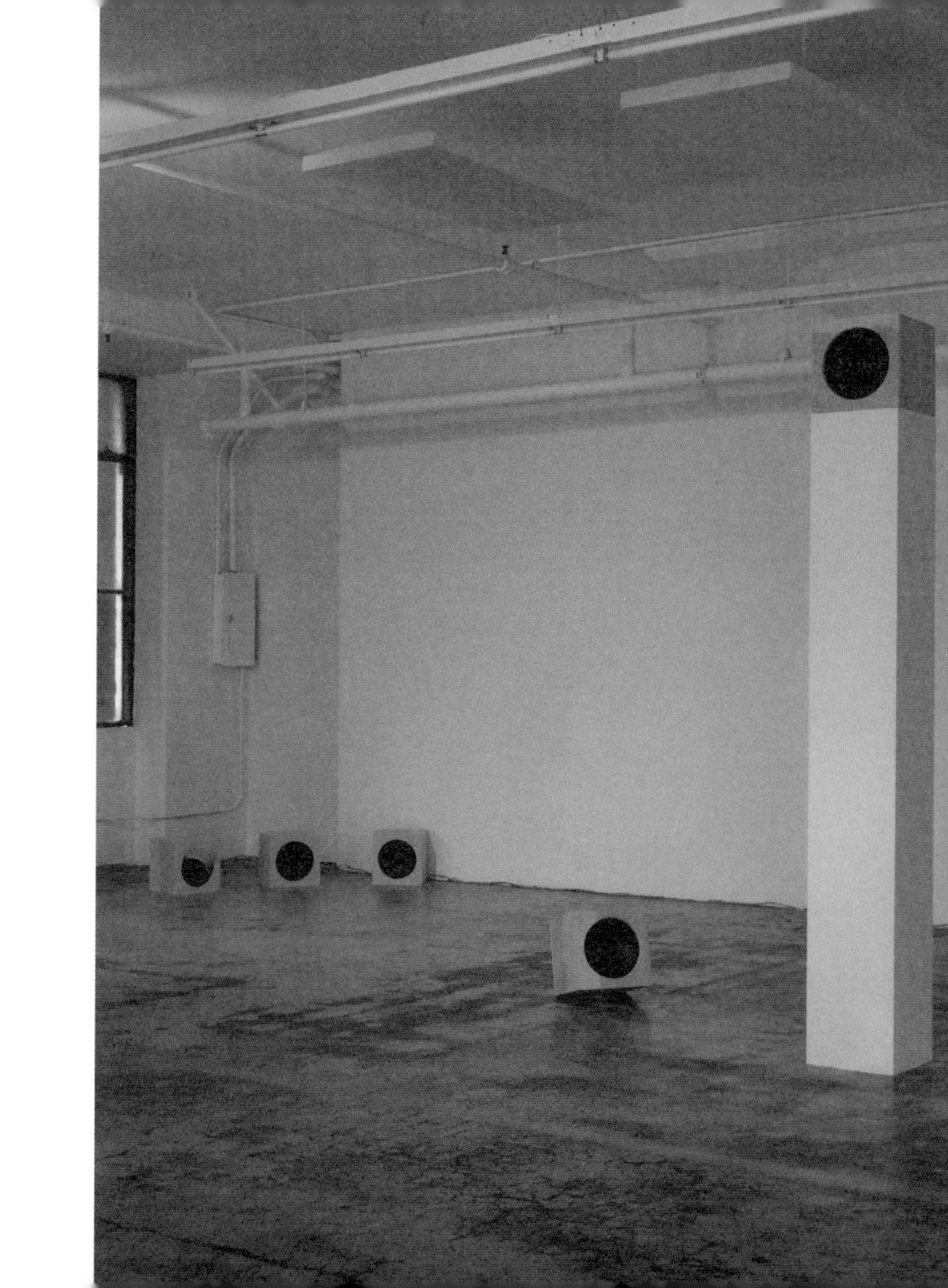

IF THE EVIL BEAST SHOULD RETURN TODAY?

ALAS, WHO IS DO CARE US NOW

AND COMFORT US? (THE SUN!)

IF RETURNS BEAST THAT ONE NOW THEN?

SPROUTING BRANCHES AND LEAVES.

SPROUTING THING BRANCHES AND LEAVES

PERHAPS IN RESPONSE TO THE LIMPID DESIRES

THE FOOTPRINTS THAT RUNNING NOW

THE BRUTAL TEETH OF HERDS

WITH ROCK GREEN PRECIOUS

JUST TO SHOW LOVE

ENJOY YOUR

FOREHEAD SITTING YOU HEAD

BUT, RATHER, GRASS DISEMBODIED.

EVEN IF YOU STRIKE ME

LET THE FINE SWANS OF DIRCE
LET THE FINE SWANS OF DIRCE
LET THE FINE SWANS OF DIRCE
LET THE FINE SWANS OF DIRCE
EVER HURT IT AGAIN.
EVER HURT IT AGAIN.

ACKNOWLEDGMENTS

I first traveled to Athens with the visionary support of Rodeo's Sylvia Kouvali in July 2021 with the intent of finishing *Dafne Phono* in two months. Her initial faith in the work spearheaded the entire production. Production took on a life of its own, not without some very challenging moments, and eventually relied on a wide network of friends to be completed, appropriately so given the work's mycelial mode. I was assisted the entire time by Sotiris Vougiatzis, whose essential skills, finesse, sense of humor, and dedication to the work made it possible. I cannot overstate their importance. Since July 2021, two installations of *Dafne Phono* have been presented, with a third forthcoming at The Museum of Modern Art in New York at the time of writing. For this, I have a lot of people to thank.

It was a gift to spend time with the speakers of the languages in the work, and to have spent time in 2021 and 2022 listening to the largest amount of language sounds in my life. In Namibia, I was hosted by, and worked with Klosi—who sometimes goes by John Barse—of the San People, on his plot in Corridor 17 in the Kalahari Desert. Franco "Franz" Tsame, also of Corridor 17, transcribed the !Xoon translations created by him, Klosi, and a shifting group of contributing villagers, and read them aloud to the other vocalists when it came time to record. Klosi's late grandfather, !Gubi, and his family have toured their own music before, performing as The !Gubi Family. Their performances are archived on YouTube, as are short films about their family, which can be found on their channel. Franco Tsame has a group called Xosil Unity, which can be found on Bandcamp. I was put in contact with Klosi through Christfried Naumann, who worked with the San to create an orthography of the Taa dialects. I have all of them to thank.

For the Chatino translation, I worked with Mexico City-based linguistic anthropologist Emiliana Cruz who was born in the Zacatepec Chatino village of Cieneguilla in the mountains of Oaxaca, Mexico. She translated the text with Claudia García, and let me stay in her home there. In Cieneguilla, Claudia García was generous with her talents and knowledge by guiding me through the village and connecting me with vocalists, as well as by being a vocalist herself.

I worked with the vocalists from the Canary Islands and Abkhazia remotely, with the help of liaisons and translators, including Nahui Garcia, a brilliant research assistant and translator of Spanish, which is the language adapted to whistle Silbo Gomero. Don Eugenio Darios, master Silbo Gomero whistler, and Dave Watts, who traveled from Tenerife to record him, were also invaluable to this opera. Darios's whistled frequencies cut through the tracks as they do through the mountains and valleys of the Canary Islands. Astan Kudzhba, an Abkhaz physicist living in Izmir, must be thanked for his enormous contribution in coordinating with vocalists and a recording studio in Abkhazia, as well as for the translation.

Thanks to Latin translator Julian Thomas Ooi, who offered a refined text. Renato Grieco came through not only as an expressive Italian vocalist, but also as one with intimate knowledge of Renaissance Italian. I have him to thank for his vivid vocal interpretation of the original libretto.

Curator Hannah Spears organized the first iteration of *Dafne Phono* at JOAN, Los Angeles, and she is largely to thank for the sound and text components of the work, having also been the one to transcribe and assemble the first version of the libretto printed here. Thanks also to JOAN Executive Director and Curator Suzy Halajian. Another printed libretto was made for the Greek presentation of the work in Piraeus, with a Greek translation by Melisanthi Giannousi.

There was a point when, after throwing multiple large-scale sculptures away due to material failure, I didn't know how I was going to continue. That's when Dirfis Manitaria, a mushroom farm in Evia, Greece, came down upon me like a deus ex machina. Dirfis' Lefteris Lahouvaris and Thanasis Mastrogiannis lent their facilities, spawn, and staff, with a spirit of generosity and curiosity. I owe them a lot.

Another stroke of good fortune came about a year into production, when money was tight and moods were tense; I was unsure if the show in Piraeus—the full iteration with monumental mycelial sculptures—was actually going to happen. I received a surprising email when I was perhaps at my lowest. Curator Sophie Cavoulacos from The Museum of Modern Art was writing to announce that she had proposed a presentation of *Dafne Phono* at MoMA, and that this proposal had been accepted. She had seen its first iteration in Los Angeles, and we'd had many conversations about it; we had met years earlier, when she asked for a studio visit after seeing my work at Miguel Abreu Gallery in 2019. I have Sophie to thank for being an advocate and interlocutor: her encouragement and resources were integral to the realization of the shows both in Greece and now at MoMA.

The initial research for this work was aided by consultations with Francesca Fantiappè and Tim Carter, foremost scholars of the original opera. The Onassis AiR program lent recording equipment for my travels thanks to Ash Bulayev. Sean McCann, my dear friend who puts out my music through his imprint Recital, and who mastered the tracks, put me in touch with forefounding sound artist Charlie Morrow, who in turn aided me in acquiring Genelec speakers for the highest quality sound through Bon Studio in Athens. A big thanks also to Dimitris Kouvalis who stepped in when I was faced with having to store many square meters worth of organic sculptures, and then coming in to help again with his talents as a lighting designer in Greece. Thanks also to Thanos Vasiliou for the steel work, Abbe Findley for traveling with me to Namibia, Alden Mackey for 3D renders and armature design assistance and love, Amy Faust for help in the studio, Samon Rajabnik for engineering my JOAN install, Despina Charitonidi for studio space, Justin Streichman for his obsessively detailed subtitle video editing, Juliette Amoroso for her obsessively detailed sound editing, Gabriel Abrantes, Mariana Antzoulatou, Negar Azimi, Emilie and David Craig, Benjamin Crotty, Ben Eastham, Panos Fourtoulakis, Suzy Halajian, Katy Green, Dakota Higgins, Georgios Koutrotsios, Ioanna Kouvali, Quinn Latimer, May Makki, Sacha and Timour Mobarak, Seidou, Froso Pini, Chris Olsen, Rhett Roback, Jamie Rollins, Pal Surinder, Basak Doga Temur, Lucy Thomason, Olga Tzogas, all the vocalists, the Foundation for Contemporary Arts for the Emergency Grant, the Nicoletta Fiorucci Foundation, Suzanna Laskaridis, Rhea Papanicolaou-Frangista, and of course the whole team at Sylvia Kouvali, and at The Museum of Modern Art.

Finally, I'm very grateful to have the opportunity to make this book and corresponding record, to properly document all that has gone into *Dafne Phono*. Thanks to Rachel Valinsky and Wendy's Subway, Scott Ponik, and Sean McCann, for sharing their own arts.

These acknowledgements read back to me, in a sense, as a chronicle of the multiple strokes of good luck that saved the project whenever I thought it might not happen. I realize that it wasn't so much good fortune as the hard work and generosity of curious, ingenious, and willing people. Here I've named just some of those who helped me directly; it would be impossible to mention everyone who informed this endeavor. I apologize to anyone I missed, and again, thanks.

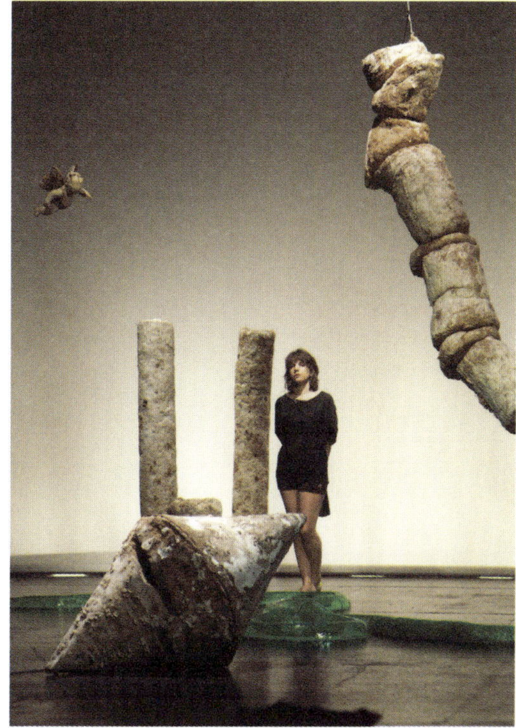

CREDITS

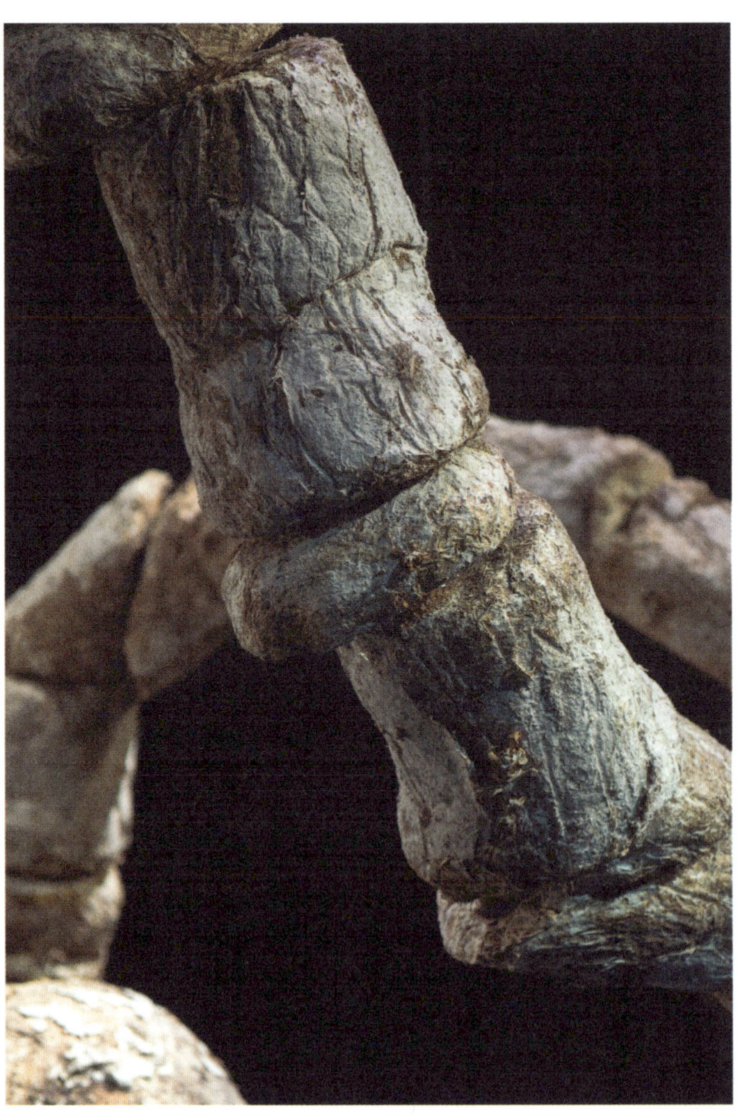

Libretto

Original Italian libretto for *Dafne* written in 1598 by Ottavio Rinuccini
Italian translation by Tim Carter, Mattia Cappelletti, Francesca Fantappiè, and Nour Mobarak
Abkhaz translation by Astan Kudzhba
Chatino translation by Emiliana Cruz and Claudia García Baltazar
Latin translation by Julian Thomas Ooi
Spanish for Silbo Gomero translation by Nahui Garcia
!Xoon translation by John Djujui Klosi Barase and Franco Tsame, with input from other denizens of Corridor 17, Namibia
Greek translation by Melissanthi Giannousi

Vocalists

Apollo: Renato Grieco (Italian)
Cupid: Arnou Argun (Abkhaz)
Dafne: Agnes |xaye (!Xoon)
Ovid: Olivia O'Dwyer (Latin)
Venus: Don Eugenio Darias (Silbo Gomero)
Abkhaz Chorus: Liana Ebzhnou, Murman Guaramia, Fatima Kharzalia, and Gunda Osia
Chatino Chorus: Felix Daniel Peña Mendes, José Vasquez Canseco, Catalina Candelario Matias, and Claudia Garcia Baltazar
!Xoon Chorus: Franco Tsame, John Djujui Klosi Barase, and Charity Tsame
Clarinet: Steve Kado

Technicians

Abkhaz recorded by Alexander Tsyamryuk
Silbo Gomero recorded by Dave Watts
!Xoon and Chatino recorded by Nour Mobarak
Latin recorded by Olivia O'Dwyer
Italian recorded by Renato Grieco
Sound engineer for post-production: Juliette Amoroso
Sound mixing and mastering: Sean McCann
Video editor: Justin Streichman
Artist assistant for *Dafne Phono*: Sotiris Vougiatzis

IMAGE CAPTIONS

Key—
All works by the artist, unless otherwise noted.
Photographer abbreviations:
Stathis Mamalkis – SM
Nour Mobarak – NM
Sotiris Vougiatzis – SV

Endpapers

pp. 1–2, 120: *Dafne Phono* (detail), 2021–2023, Municipal Theatre of Piraeus, Athens, July 20–September 16, 2023. Courtesy the artist and Sylvia Kouvali. Photo: SM

p. 119: *Cosey*, 2023, *Trametes versicolor* mycelium and glass beads. Courtesy the artist and Sylvia Kouvali. Photo: NM

Preface

pp. 9–10: *Gods' Facsimiles*, installation view, Rodeo Piraeus, London, June 2–September 23, 2023. Courtesy the artist and Sylvia Kouvali. Photo: Deniz Guzel

p. 11: *Dafne Phos,* 2022 (detail). Etched colored glass. Installation view, *SIREN (some poetics)*, Amant Foundation, Brooklyn, New York, September 15, 2022–March 5, 2023. Courtesy the artist, Amant, and Sylvia Kouvali. Photo: Adrianna Glaviano

p. 13: *Dafne Phono*, 2021–2023, installation view, Municipal Theatre of Piraeus, Athens, July 20–September 16, 2023. Courtesy the artist and Sylvia Kouvali. Photo: SM

Process

p. 18: (top, left) Detail of *Apollo* sculpture skirt relief, adapted from Bernardo Buontalenti's sketches of the original costumes. Photo: SM; (top, right) Clay positive of *Apollo*: A plastic and plaster mold was made from this positive to grow *Apollo*'s final form. Photo: NM; (bottom, left) Clay positive of *Python*. Photo: NM; (bottom, right) Detail of *Python*. Photo: NM

p. 19: Fan growing in the studio in Athens. Photo: NM

p. 20: The artist with works-in-progress in the studio, Athens. Photo: SV

p. 21: (top, left) Pressure-cooking grain substrate for sterilization in the mycelium growing process; (top, right and bottom, left) Glaraki Street 10B Studio, Athens; (bottom, right) Final works in studio storage, depicting *Venus*'s armature, among other works. All photos: NM

p. 22: (top, left) Grow bag production line, Dirfis Manitaria, Euboea, Greece. Photo: NM; (top, right); Temperature- and humidity-controlled growing silo, Dirfis Manitaria. Photo: NM; (bottom, left) Grow bag production line, Dirfis Manitaria. Photo: NM; (bottom, right) Artist with *Chorus* in dehydration silo, Dirfis Manitaria. Photo: SV

p. 23: *Chorus* in dehydration silo, Dirfis Manitaria. Photo: NM

p. 24: *Dafne* in the studio, Athens. Photo: NM

p. 25: (top, left and middle) *Dafne* growing at Dirfis Manitaria. Photo: NM; (top, right) *Dafne,* work-in-progress in the studio, Athens. Photo: NM; (bottom, left) Mobarak shaping *Dafne* with Athanasios Mastrogiannis, co-founder of Dirfis Manitaria (standing, back), and two members of Dirfis staff—Stavros Mastrogiannis (crouching, back) and Parveen Singh (right). Photo: SV; (bottom, right) Assistant Sotiris Vougiatzis and welder Thanos Vasiliou assembling *Dafne* in the studio, Athens. Photo: NM

p. 26: Glass beads stitched into cardboard and placed in jars for the pressure sterilization process, before being set into mycelium substrate. The mycelium eats the cardboard, leaving the glass beads inlaid in the surface of the sculptures. Photo: NM

p. 27: (left) *Cupid*; (right) All of *Dafne Phono's* sculptural components. Both photos: NM

Characters

p. 28: (top, left): *Dafne Copy,* 2023. *Trametes versicolor* mycelium, glass beads, string (45 × 50 × 20 cm), wood plaster (100 × 120 × 50 cm); (top, right): *Apollo Copy,* 2023. *Trametes versicolor* mycelium (30 × 25 × 30 cm), wood plaster (100 × 120 × 50 cm). Courtesy the artist and Sylvia Kouvali. Photo: SM

p. 52: (top, left) *Venus Copy,* 2023. *Trametes versicolor* mycelium, glass beads, string, watercolor paint (65 × 23 × 23 cm), wood plaster (100 × 120 × 50 cm); (top, right) *Cupid Copy,* 2023. *Trametes versicolor* mycelium, glass beads (32 cm × 45 cm × 32 cm), wood plaster (100 × 120 × 50 cm). Courtesy the artist and Sylvia Kouvali. Photo: SM

p 82: (top, left) *Python Copy,* 2023. Resin, 59.5 × 188 × 10 cm; (top, middle) *Chorus Copy*, 2023. Nine *Pleurotus citrinopileatus* mycelium columns (90 × 8 × 8 cm); (top, right) *Ovid Copy*, Hole, wood plaster, 100 × 120 × 50 cm. All courtesy the artist and Sylvia Kouvali. Photo: SM; (bottom, right) *Ovid Copy*, 2022. Hole, wood plaster, 100 × 120 × 50 cm. Courtesy the artist and Sylvia Kouvali. Photo: Deniz Guzel

pp. 28, 52, 82: (bottom) Sketches of original costumes for Dafne, Apollo, Venus, Cupid, and Python for Ottavio Rinuccini and Jacopo Peri's opera, *Dafne* (1598). Illustrations by Bernardo Buontalenti. Courtesy Biblioteca Nazionale Centrale di Firenze.

Libretto

pp. 48–49: "Rappresentazione di Dafne: Favola pastorale composta dal signor Ottavio Rinuccini. Et fatta recitare in musica dal Signor Iacopo Corsi" (1598). Courtesy Music Division, The New York Public Library, New York Public Library Digital Collections. Accessed September 8, 2024, https://digitalcollections.nypl.org/items/9635f75d-ff6e-6929-e040-e00a18061b4b.

pp. 50–51: Pages from !Xoon translation process, transcribed by Franco Tsame.

Dafne Phono, installation Images

pp. 72–80: *Dafne Phono*, 2021–2023. Installation, *Pleurotus citrinopileatus* and *Trametes versicolor* mycelium, glass beads, watercolor paint, wood, plaster, PET plastic, silicone, steel, vacuum, hole (11 × 7 cm), 15-channel sound, single-channel video (22 min), dimensions variable. Installation view, Municipal Theatre of Piraeus, Athens, July 20–September 16, 2023. Courtesy the artist and Sylvia Kouvali. Photo: SM

p. 81: *Fans* (22 total): *Bernadette, Billie, Brandy, Chaka, Cicciolina, Cookie, Cosey, Divine, Emilie, Geneva Jaccuzzi, Isabella Andreini, Jack Smith, Madonna, Mae, Maria, Mariah, Miyako, Nina, Prince, Rupaul, Sylvia, Whitney*, 2021–2023. *Trametes versicolor* mycelium, glass beads, acrylic paint, dimensions variable. Courtesy the artist and Sylvia Kouvali. Photo: SM

pp. 104–105: *Dafne Phono*, 2022. 16-channel sound installation, 16 speakers in artist's birch and red oak speaker cabinets, glass beads, 7-ft. plinth, vacuum, hole (11 × 7 cm), video (22 min). Installation view, JOAN, Los Angeles, June 30–August 27, 2022. Courtesy the artist, JOAN, and Sylvia Kouvali. Photo: Josh Schaedel

Dafne Phono, video

pp. 106–111: *Dafne Phono*, 2022 (stills). Single-channel video with English subtitles, 22 min, color, sound. Courtesy the artist and Sylvia Kouvali.

Acknowledgments and Credits

pp. 113: Portrait of Nour Mobarak in *Dafne Phono*, Municipal Theatre of Piraeus, Athens, July 27, 2023. Photo: Anastasia Perahia

pp. 114: *Dafne Phono* (detail), 2021–2023, Municipal Theatre of Piraeus, Athens, July 20–September 16, 2023. Courtesy the artist and Sylvia Kouvali. Photo: Anastasia Perahia

Dafne Phono

"Translation and Metamorphosis"

Document Series #11
First Edition, 2024
Edition of 1,000 copies
ISBN: 979-8-9909878-3-8
LCCN: 2024943865

Edited by Rachel Valinsky
Design by Scott Ponik
Image retouching by Michel Sixou
Typeset in Optima LT, Times New Roman, and Arial Vertical Blinds
Printed at Jelgavas Tipogrāfija, Latvia

Distributed in the USA
by Asterism Books
asterismbooks.com

Distributed in the UK / Europe
by Antenne Books
antennebooks.com

Published by Wendy's Subway
379 Bushwick Avenue
Brooklyn, NY 11206
wendyssubway.com

Wendy's Subway is a non-profit reading room, writing space, and independent publisher located in Brooklyn.

The Document Series is an interdisciplinary publishing initiative that highlights work by time-based artists in printed form.

The Document Series is supported, in part, by the National Endowment for the Arts, and by public funds from the New York City Department of Cultural Affairs in Partnership with the City Council.

Dafne Phono is supported, in part, by a Foundation for Contemporary Arts Emergency Grant; Sylvia Kouvali, London/Piraeus; the Nicoletta Fiorucci Foundation; Suzanna Laskaridis; and Rhea Papanicolaou-Frangista. The book is published on the occasion of the exhibition *Dafne Phono* at The Museum of Modern Art, New York, October 26, 2024–January 12, 2025, and accompanied by an album, released by Recital. Special thanks to Sophie Cavoulacos and May Makki, The Museum of Modern Art, New York, and Sean McCann, Recital.

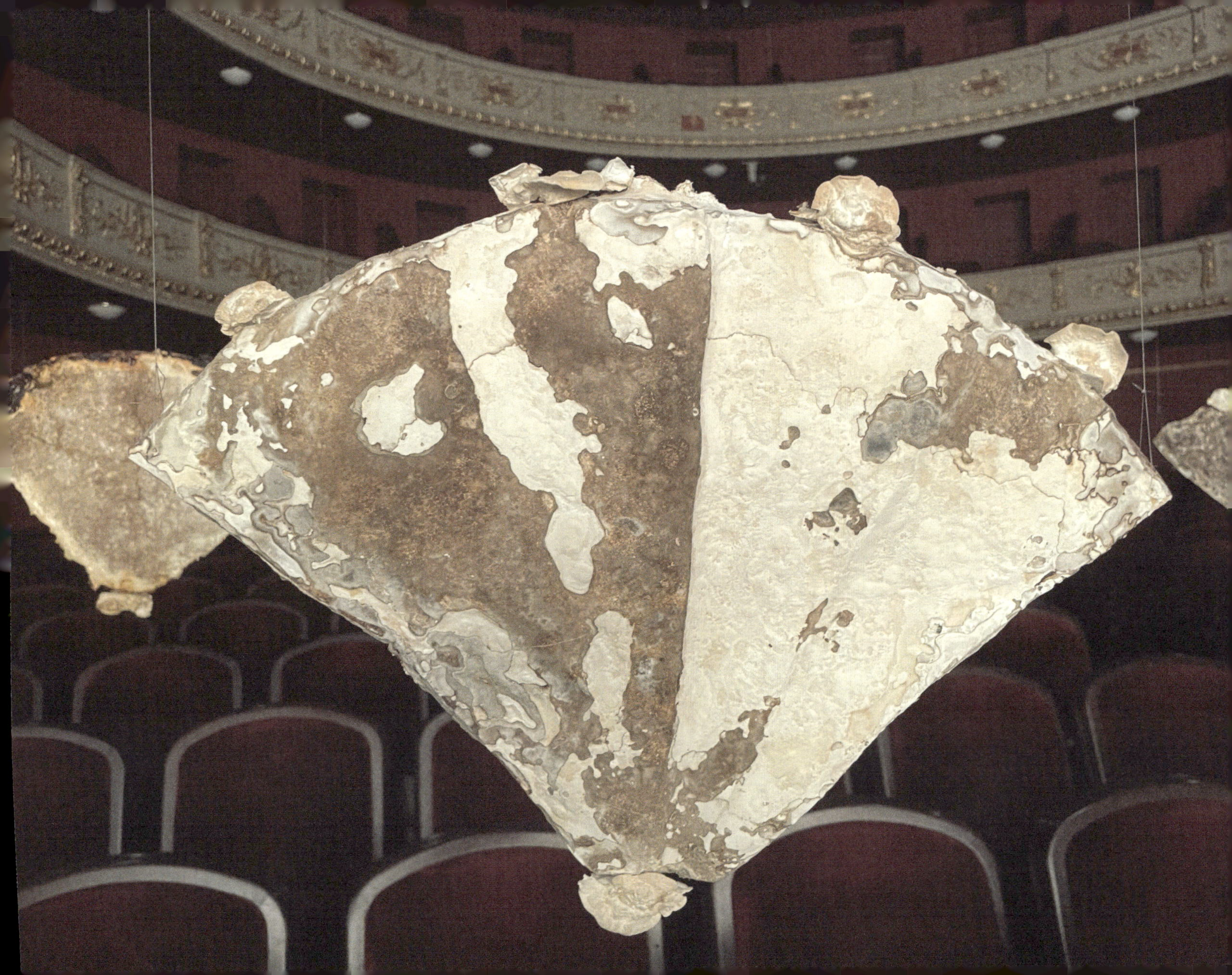

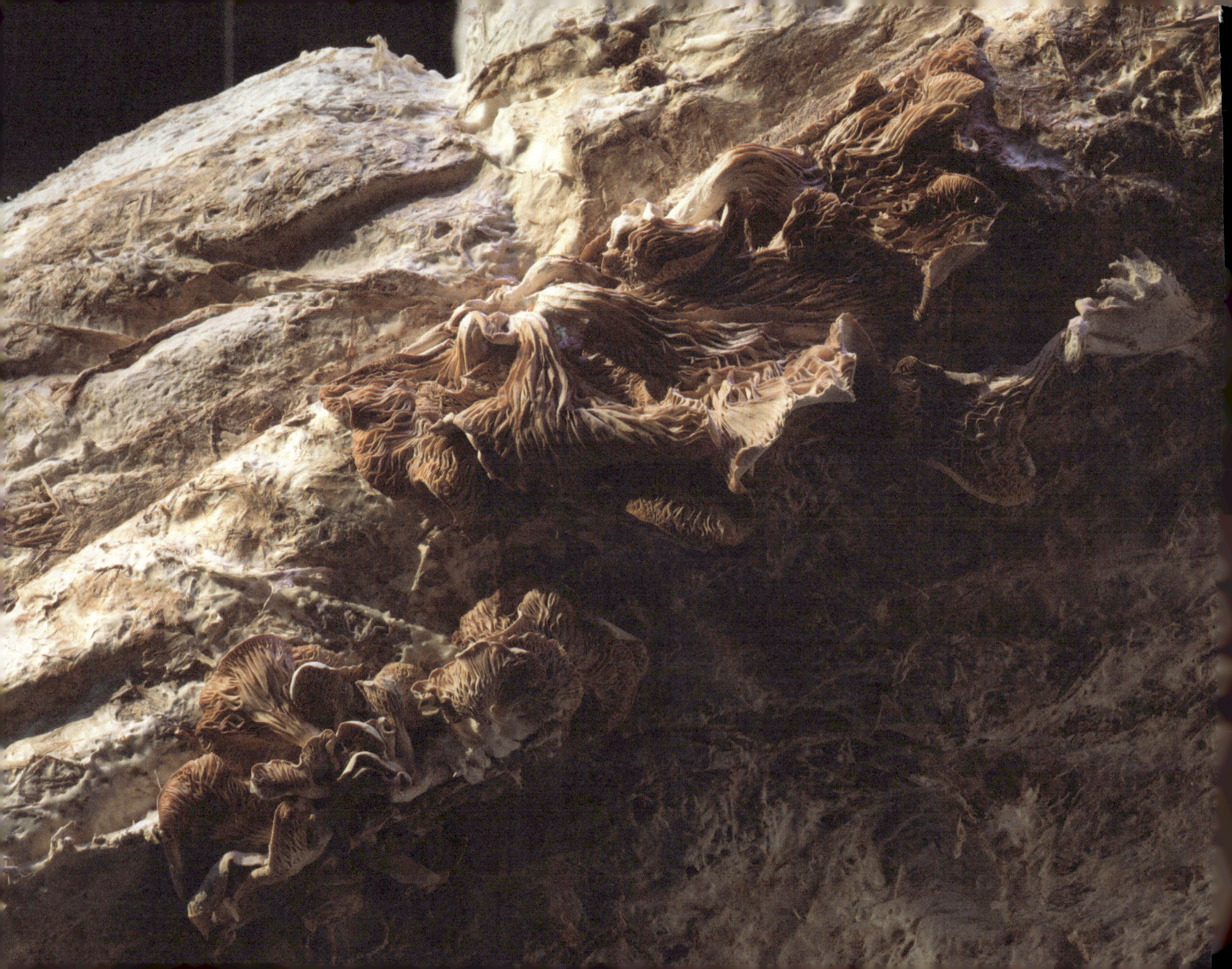